*Dedicated to those who
endured and survived
the Great Depression*

———■———

# MY FOLKS'
# DEPRESSION DAYS

*A Treasury of Great Depression Stories*
*Shared By Capper's Readers*

Capper Press
Topeka, Kansas

Illustration, Design and Production:
Diana J. Edwardson Persell

Editor:
Michele R. Webb

ISBN: 0-941678-40-7

# FOREWORD

"Use it up, wear it out, make it do, or do without," is the dominant theme of these treasured memories of the Great Depression, shared by *Capper's* readers in 1993. After a call went out for personal memories of the Depression, folks recorded their triumphs, heartbreaks and hard-time survival tips as learning tools for a new generation. This book is the sequel to the dynamic *My Folks And The One-Room Schoolhouse*, and continues the dynamic *My Folks* series. The series began with *My Folks Came In A Covered Wagon* and *My Folks Claimed The Plains*, treasuries of stories from the pioneer and homesteading eras.

Another theme stressed in this collection of letters is that of pulling together, not only as families, but also as communities. There was no such thing as a stranger, due to the appearances of traveling salesmen and down-on-their-luck transients who often had nothing but the clothes on their back. Trust was a common reaction to those around you. Often "one man's trash" was "another man's treasure" as every article of daily life was used and re-used so that nothing went to waste.

Our goal with this treasury of personal recollections is to share the spirit of the times with those who did not live them. It was essential that the stories be collected, not only to convey that hard times can be survived with times of happiness, but also hard times can be avoided by future generations. In a time of technology and plenty, it is beneficial to preserve the heritage of simplicity and need that was the Great Depression.

We make no claim of complete historical accuracy, but offer this as a personal glimpse into the past as it is remembered by those who lived it. I have, in an attempt to maintain the authentic flavor of the stories, made few spelling, punctuation or grammatical corrections.

We thank and salute our contributors, who made it possible for us to share this era with a new generation of readers.

Michele Webb
Editor

History informs us
That through the ages,
Ever so often
A panic rages.

But we must not think
Of our country's past,
We must find some way
To make this the last.

We must endeavor
And try hard to plan,
Ways to stop panics
That cover our land.

We must all try
Our honor to save
And drive all panics
Down to their grave.
                    1933
                    Helen Warner
                    North Kansas City, Missouri

# CONTENTS

# CHAPTER 1:  Signs Of The Times

### "Use It Up, Wear It Out, Make It Do, Or Do Without"

I remember the GREAT DEPRESSION.  I was a twelve-year-old farm kid in arid Western Kansas in 1929 when the stock market collapsed, and the money movers in Wall Street jumped out of skyscraper windows.  This universal financial debacle probably had less effect on our part of the country and our neighbors than on most of the rest of the world.  We were already short of cash because crops hadn't been good and farm prices were down.  So we went from very little hard cash to virtually none, as did most all the people we knew.  All of us were in the same leaky boat!  Farm communities re-developed a sort of pioneer self-sufficiency.

In our family, we were never hungry, because we had the usual farm animals (cows, chickens, and hogs) plus a vegetable garden.  A balanced diet was not always possible, but we surely had enough to eat.

Clothing was a different matter.  Buying replacement shoes and overalls was difficult because of the lack of cash.  The "use it up, wear it out, make it do, or do without" philosophy quickly became a way of life.

Shelter was probably the least difficult of the three basic requirements for my parents to provide.  We had a house on the farm, so we were out of the weather.  However, fuel for cooking and heating in the winter months could be a problem. In that part of the state there were very few trees, so whatever wood there was had been imported from timbered areas for use as fenceposts or as lumber. After all the old fenceposts and scrap lumber had been burned, we had to turn to the standard fuel of the prairie - cow chips!

Given the state of the economy with so little money in circulation, the barter system came into play. Fresh produce and dairy products could sometimes be swapped for food staples, hardware items or clothing. Neighbors helped each other (as they always had) with major tasks such as building repair, harvesting crops, butchering animals for meat, breaking horses and overhauling machinery. Eventually, Federal Government programs such as WPA, CCC, NRA and other "Roosevelt acronyms," provided some relief in the form of jobs and paychecks. However, being "on relief" was unacceptable to most of the population; it was very important that these jobs were not a form of dole, but the people actually performed useful tasks for those small paychecks. For example, Dad got a WPA job with a team of his horses on construction of an earth dam about 15 miles from home. Dad would leave home long before daylight, driving the team and wagon to the construction site to arrive before the day's work began. He had the same trip at night, so he got home well after dark.

A series of dry years in the early '30s accentuated the hard times in this part of the state. Crop yields were very low because of the drought. Grain prices were at a historic low. There was not enough hay and grain to feed the animal population. All this made it necessary for farmers, like we were, to borrow money for seed for new crops, and for feed for our animals. There were Federal loan programs to bail us out temporarily, but we had successive dry years and it was pretty bleak for a while. The government feed and seed loans were eventually satisfied, but they were a cloud on the farm family finances for a long time.

Rex O. Wonnell
San Jose, California

## State Of The Nation

A depression does not arrive on a specific day, various economic indicators are evident some years earlier. My dad often discussed neighboring farmer friends losing their land at the conclusion of World War I when commodity prices dropped, making it impossible for them to pay for land that they had purchased at an inflated $600.00 per acre, and they also lost their original smaller farms around 1920.

A new neighbor persuaded my dad to buy the new Fordor Ford Sedan in 1923 for $750.00, but he didn't like that car so he traded it in on a new 1924 model 4-cylinder Buick which was $1,040.00. Then dad bought a new 1924 Fordson Tractor including a new Oliver two bottom breaking plow for $465.00 total. There was no sales tax in that era. In 1925 my mother bought a Kodak folding 2 A Brownie Camera at F. M. Leslie's store for $9.50, reduced from $10.00 the preceding week when the War Tax from World War I was taken off such items. Prices are given to indicate values on what I remember of a bygone era.

F.M. Leslie's store was closed when he went broke, and the bank beside it had failed. Mom met an old neighbor coming out of the bank so he told us that this was the saddest day of his life, because bank regulators required all stockholders to sign over all of their properties, so he lost his farm.

We had little idea of the impending depression other than my dad grumbling about $8.00 for a fat hog. A grain elevator went bankrupt so my dad lost around $400.00, being as unsold grain always goes into the bankruptcy settlement, so he got nothing. Remember, that was nearly the price of a new tractor. On dollar day Robeson's sold Headlight brand bib overalls for $1.00 per pair, so dad bought a pile high enough to last for a year. We knew nothing of designer labels, we didn't have a new faded look, and bought a larger size due to shrinkage, because Sanforizing was not known. Blue chambray shirts were 75¢, canton flannel husking gloves were 98¢ per dozen, a 100 lb. bag of potatoes was $1.00, a 48 lb. bag of flour was in a cloth bag for 98¢, and a 100 lb. bag of sugar was $4.00 in a cloth bag inside a strong burlap bag. My dad's lost grain could have bought a lot of things.

The 1928 election concealed the hard times. Republican candidate Herbert Hoover talked of two cars in every garage, and prosperity was just around the corner. My dad was a fourth generation Democrat, and I well remember a neighbor man yelling at me in glee that my dad's candidate had lost, but that man's joy was short-lived.

A bank on the north side of Main Street in Urbana failed in 1929, and it reached right into my school class. The president of the bank was prosecuted, and sent to prison, but his son continued to school for awhile. We were not affected at home by the bank failure, but some depositors lost their life savings, and one committed suicide. The bank president was sent to prison for eight years, and everyone in the community was upset that a man who stole chickens to feed his starving family received fifteen years in prison, a travesty of justice. Lester L. Corrie, being an Urbana businessman, persuaded banks to close for a week. He had Urbana Money printed which was guaranteed redeemable at face value, so I remember we used some of it until the banks reopened.

I can't really say that the Stock Market Crash of 1929 had any immediate effect on us. The Republicans and the Democrats were blaming each other for the hard times. Franklin Delano Roosevelt was a convincing orator so he won the election in an overwhelming landslide. Men who held State jobs were dismissed to make way for Democrats.

March 20, 1933, brought widespread changes when Roosevelt was sworn into his first term as President of the United States. A moratorium on banks was ordered, all were closed to begin reforms, Mom said we had $2.00 in cash in the house, but we did survive. Bank deposits came in under the Federal Deposit Insurance Corporation, abbreviated FDIC, which is still very much in effect. A depositor who has less than $100,000.00 is insured for the full amount. A bank may close, making it very inconvenient for him for a few days, but he will get back every cent.

The inaugural of President Roosevelt was barely over when Congress repealed the Volstead Act, more commonly known as Prohibition, or the selling of liquor in the United States. The very first day that taverns were permitted to sell liquor, some high school boys skipped school. Not one was past eighteen. I didn't waste time or money on it.

The darkest days of the depression came during Roosevelt's first year. People were in severe financial straits, jobless and broke. Sweeping changes for farmers did keep some from losing their farms. There was a corn hog program which was controversial. When city folks were starving, pigs were killed, and bodies were burned or buried to bring hog prices up to a profit. My dad would not participate. He continued the same way he had operated all of his life. We got no government subsidies at all. Others did get subsidies.

Getting a job was impossible from the farm, so the government had the Civilian Conservation Corps established. No chance for my dad, because he had land, but his cousin's son got to go because he was only a hired farmhand. It was called CCC.

President Roosevelt spoke frequently on the radio, referred to as Fireside Chats. One was memorable. He said to all farmers in danger of losing their farms, "You write me a letter tonight giving particulars, and I will see what I can do to save the farm."

The NRA was signed into law by President Hoover in his last year, so President Roosevelt implemented it under the true name of The National Recovery Act. Evidences were in store windows where participating businesses displayed posters NRA with a Blue Eagle emblem under which was printed BUY AMERICAN in large letters until World War II broke out.

Did anyone foretell the depression? Certainly, noted economist Roger Babson had predicted it, but was ignored. Nobody would have ever heard of him if the depression had never occurred.

I claim the depression lasted into World War II.

I have learned that the youth should listen to their loving

5

parents, grandparents and older people for some words of wisdom. Those people should also listen carefully to their children, they might learn something.

Emmett Kirby
Champaign, Illinois

## Paid In Oats

Our first child was born in December of 1930, and the doctor bill was twenty-five dollars. Of course we didn't have electricity, and the wind mill pumped our water - when the wind blew. Kerosene for our lamp was 10¢ a gallon.

We hired a man to help pick corn (which was 10¢ a bushel) for one cent a bushel, and did not have the money to pay him the dollar a day he made. The next summer he came and got his $8.00 in oats.

Ethel M. Tuttle
Clear Lake, Iowa

## Four New Dresses

I was a child during the depression. One of the things I remember my mother considered a bargain was when the grocery store she traded at would have six cans of Van Camp's pork and beans for a quarter. One time she was able to get a yellow glass plate for a penny by buying some food items. This was a pretty plate with a design in the glass and she always used it for placing a home baked cake on it. It was depression-ware glass. I still have it in my possession some sixty years later. Handling things carefully and taking care of everything is still what I do all these many years later.

One time our local J.C. Penny store had girl's ready-made cotton dresses piled up on a counter at four for $1.00. Mother decided she couldn't make them that cheap so she bought them for me. I wore them until I outgrew them. I never had four new dresses before so I thought it was wonderful. Merchandise was priced so low during the depression, but wages were extremely low if one was fortunate enough to have a job.

Mary Scott
Oklahoma City, Oklahoma

## "What Can't Be Cured"

My grandmother had a saying I heard often, "What Can't Be Cured Must Be Endured." That was true them and just as true now.

Jane Curtis Waldroop
Norman, Oklahoma

## Price Comparisons

I was a teenager during the Depression. We had our phone taken out, which was $3.00 a month. The electricity was $8.50 a month and it was disconnected, so back to kerosene lamps.

In 1932 corn was 21¢ a bushel and only 15 to 20 bushels an acre. In 1936 hamburger was 10¢ a pound, 3 cans of corn 29¢, ten pounds of flour was 43¢, a quart of milk was 10¢, eggs were 19¢ a dozen, and a rib roast was 25¢ a pound.

I bought a $1,000.00 life insurance policy and the premiums were $6.23 every three months. My brother bought a used car for $600.00. The monthly payments were $15.00, and I gave him $5.00 a month.

By this time things were getting better, war had been declared. I had the phone installed at the farm and the electricity was turned on again.

Ruth M. DeBuse
Omaha, Nebraska

## Wedding Gifts

My future sister-in-law and my mother and I went to Omaha to buy our wedding dresses. Rose and I were both married in 1935. I bought a white satin gown for $12.50. I already had a pair of white shoes to go with it. I sewed a long slip to wear with the gown. I did not buy a veil because we were watching every penny.

A bridal shower brought many useful gifts. They included towels, tablecloths, rolling pin, water bucket and dipper. Also were dishes, pans, and a wash basin which were useful as there were no homes with running water.

My parents furnished me with a Sears rotary sewing machine, bedroom and dining room furniture, a gasoline powered washing machine and a quick meal stove that burned wood and cobs.

Later my husband's parents gave us 60 white hens. My parents gave us 100 baby chicks and an oil burning brooder stove, and four young Holstein cows.

We somehow survived five more years of drouth.

Ella Travnicek
Cedar Bluffs, Nebraska

## Depressions

Depression is here
Depression is there
Depressin it seem,
Is just everywhere.

Depressions have come
Depressions will go.
They've been here before
And they've left, we know.

One hundred years past,
A panic was had,
We call this terrible
But one was bad.

Our debts with foreigners
Are reversed somehow.
We owe them money
But they owe us now.

Ere to depressions,

The country seems fine,
'Men don't realize
There'll be a hard time.

And when they do come,
Men rant and they rave
They try every scheme
Their country to save.

But time takes its course
And in a few years,
Depression is gone
And so are man's fears.

History shows clearly,
Theat it takes five years,
Before a panc,
Really disappears.

Of course it takes time
For panics to go,
Their details are kept
In history we know.

                    Helen Warner
                    North Kansas City, Missouri

## The Party Line

During the Depression we trusted everyone and they trusted you. No one was crooked.

The telephone was a crank type and on the wall. There were several neighbors on the same line. One could tell others were listening as the receiver would click. No one used a phone for business. Sometimes several neighbors would get on together and visit a bit. But I think that phone cost all of a $1.00 per month. If your phone did not work properly a service man would come and put in two new batteries that would run the phone. No charge for that.

Once in awhile our grocer would put a sack of cookies or candy in our groceries as a surprise. This was a big treat to the whole family and no charge for what he had done.

The five and ten cent stores were so enchanting to my sister and I. One counter was jewelry and a clerk at each counter and no taxes back then.

Our entertainment was most every day life. But in good weather someone would go to town and get a big chunk of ice. We then would crank an ice cream freezer and make ice cream.

Bonita DePue<br>Nevada, Missouri

## School Days

It was 1929 when I entered Urbana High School. School rental books were unknown so I began with about $8.00 worth of new books. The most expensive book I ever bought was a sophomore English book at $2.20. Once I got acquainted, I could buy secondhand textbooks for half the new price they paid, and if third hand half of what they paid. The secondhand geometry book was a bargain being as the cover was ripped open to hold a compass and a ruler. Locker charge was $1.00 per year. The cafeteria prices were more than I was told, and the neighbor said to use the lunch line for 5¢ hamburgers and 5¢ half pints of milk in glass bottles. We did not have drugs in lockers, they were unknown, but two kids may have boasted to impress us claiming they were taking three or four aspirins daily.

Depression lunch room prices were 25¢ for a plate lunch, and 45¢ for a T-bone steak dinner. Kuhn's sold Jarman dress shoes for $4.00 per pair, dress shirts were $1.29 each and a three-piece suit was $18.00.

Emmett Kirby<br>Champaign, Illinois

## CHAPTER 2: Hearty Fare

### No Loss Of Molasses

I was born in 1929, the baby girl in a family of seven brothers. I was the last, 'cause how in the world could they feed another mouth?

Our meat dishes were fish, squirrel and rabbit. Early on we didn't sacrifice our laying hens because we needed those for eggs.

A rooster was more apt to get in the pot. Sometimes he was old enough to be tough.

One year, to our great appreciation, we had a seven-gallon can of molasses, which might be a winter's supply and a valued food commodity. One of my brothers scampering up to get into the attic stepped on the lid of the molasses can. The lid slipped and down went his foot into the molasses.

Did we eat the valued molasses that winter? Of course. We lost very little molasses after the foot was removed.

Loraine Sands<br/>Lockwood, Missouri

### Country Breakfasts

When I was a little girl in the Depression years, country breakfasts are the meals that I most remember!

During the corn-husking season my parents used a home smoke-cured ham to feed the men who walked out in the dark each day. Along with the slice of ham, my mother served fried potatoes, eggs and biscuits, milk and coffee. What filling food!

In the winter, just after the "beef butchering" day in the barnyard, we would eat fresh, fried liver every meal until it was used up. Winter mornings when my Dad didn't have to hurry out to do the chores, he liked to cook breakfast. Choosing to slice some of the fresh beef-steak from the carcass, hanging high in the rafters in the freezing cold shed, my Dad often served delicious cubed-steak with man-made milk gravy (spread thick and wide) over a giant-size slice of home-made white bread.

Frequent times, in late evenings, Dad would coax my Mom to cook a kettle of corn-meal and make mush. This she would pat down in a loaf pan and then slice it in the morning and fry each piece. We put sorghum syrup on the golden hunk of mush to make our early morning meal.

I cannot remember that we ever had fruit juice, omelets, a blueberry muffin or citrus on our breakfast menu in the Depression years. We had enough to eat of what my parents raised on the farm.

Our enormous breakfasts served their double-duty: most winter days only two meals were prepared for the family.

During the Depression years, one mother of five daughters made biscuits every morning of the year to save their bread. Another lady made pancakes 365 days of the year to feed breakfast to 10 children. Our beefsteak-breakfasts were exotic!

Hope Robinson<br>Yale, Iowa

## Mainstays Of The Menu

The depression in full force, gaunt faces peered from under tattered "sock caps" and patched faded bib overalls hung from bony shoulders. Pop was tall, but now so thin he appeared even taller as Bud and I reared back to look at him. Our once chubby frames were also thin and bony. Three recipes had become the mainstays of the menu in our community during this time, regardless of the breadwinner's occupation.

Mush consisted of home-grown corn, ground at a nearby mill

into meal, sprinkled into slightly salted boiling water and stirred continuously until thickened and well done. Addition of butter, cream and sugar made a delicious dish. Omit them and you have just what the name sounds like. Leftover mush (if any) was sliced and fried for another meal.

Poor Do was originally called Chuckwagon Hash. Pioneers served this when no wild game or local flora could be found on the trail. No leftovers or scraps were ever discarded, but combined with water and a sprinkling of salt over the campfire. Cornmeal was sprinkled in and stirred constantly until thick, in the versatile iron kettle.

Soakie was a leftover biscuit or piece of cornbread split open upon a plate; sugar, if available, was sprinkled over and a small amount of boiled coffee poured on. If there was no sugar, sorghum or honey made it nutritious and filling. Extra biscuits were sometimes baked ahead and purposely used this way, especially on wash day.

Puppy Cup, another version of Soakie, was mainly for adults as young children were not allowed that much coffee. The top and bottom crusts were removed from biscuits and stacked in the cup of coffee after cream from the springhouse and sugar had been liberally stirred in. The soft biscuit centers were used to "sop" the usual milk gravy, sometimes the only semblance to meat on the table for weeks at a time.

Virginia Snyder
Bismarck, Missouri

## Beans From Sears

In the early part of this century I lived on a big farm in the southern Illinois prairie. One dish served almost daily by my mother, our neighbors, too, was navy beans. They were the same as Great Northern beans on today's grocery shelves. At that time my mother ordered beans from Sears & Roebuck. They were shipped by train in a burlap bushel sack. Soaked overnight, then cooked slowly in a large iron pot that fit the opening when a lid was removed from the big old cookstove; seasoned with pork and a big onion, they made a hearty and tasty dish always welcomed by the hired hands who were there most of the year.

I cook beans today and try to recapture that hearty flavor but they are never the same, never as good.

Florence Palmer
Paris, Illinois

## No Seconds On Potatoes

Here is a cake I often stir up and bake - it's just as delicious tasting now as it was years ago.

**"POOR MAN'S CAKE"**

About ½ cup oleo or shortening

1 cup brown sugar - beat these until smooth. Then add:

2 eggs and 2 cups fresh chopped apples.

Now beat until smooth in texture. Then add enough flour plus 1 teaspoon baking soda, some cinnamon and nutmeg, if available, until you have a firm batter. Last add 1 teaspoon vanilla and a couple handfulls of raisins. Pour into a greased pan - bake in a moderate oven until done (about 35 minutes). When cool, cut into nice size slices, eat and enjoy! It's delicious and nourishing.

We ate lots of potatoes at our home - fried, boiled, baked, soup or hash. Mashed potatoes were always served every Sunday. I don't recall anyone ever saying "Potatoes again."

When I recall these memories I wonder how in the world our mother and the other ladies managed. Now I realize they were very special people.

Matilda (Winters) Cardin
Englewood, Colorado

## Favorite Recipes

In 1941, we moved into a drafty old farmhouse that was really uncomfortable in the wintertime. Our potatoes froze behind the heating stove, and there was ice in the fishbowl. The wood heater had a flat top. I had to use it for a cookstove. My husband's hours were irregular, so I had to use recipes that would stay hot and still be palatable. One of my favorites was Beef Stew with Cornmeal Dumplings: bread, meat and vegetables all in one pot.

My husband had a sweet tooth, and since I couldn't bake cakes and pies, Dessert Dumplings with Caramel Sauce was one of his favorites. Parsley Potato Dumplings were good with soup and also made a hearty meal.

During the winter months the hens didn't lay and we were without eggs. Therefore, we were always on the lookout for "eggless" recipes. It was unheard of for farmers to buy eggs! We found that many of the recipes were acceptable without eggs. We hadn't heard of cholesterol or that there was danger of salmonella in raw eggs. Most of the old recipes called for lard, cream and butter and we were unaware that they were "hazardous to our health!"

During the depression, we didn't buy anything that could be made at home! I had a notebook that I copied recipes in, and it contains a lot of information, how to make Shampoo, Varnish Remover, Wallpaper Paste, Library Paste, a Cinder Plant and even remedies for Calf Scours and Ear Canker! Many of the old recipes called for sorghum and honey, especially during the time of sugar rationing. We also made use of wild game and fish.

## HONEY CAKE
    1   cup sour cream
    1   cup honey
    2   eggs

Mix well. Sift together 2 cups flour, 1 teaspoon baking powder, ½ teaspoon soda. Add to other ingredients, add 1 teaspoon vanilla. Mix well and bake in moderate oven until top springs back when lightly touched.

## ECONOMY PIE
    ⅔  cup vinegar
    1   cup sugar
    1   cup hot water
    2   egg yolks

2    tablespoons corn starch
Butter size of an egg

Mix vinegar, sugar, cornstarch and egg yolks until smooth, stir into boiling water. Stir constantly until it thickens. Pour into baked pie shell. Cool and top with meringue made with the 2 egg whites.

## MOCK ANGEL FOOD CAKE
1    cup scalded milk

Mix together 1 cup flour, 1 cup sugar, 3 level teaspoons baking powder, ½ teaspoon salt and sift well. Stir into scalded milk. Fold in 3 stiffly-beaten egg whites. Bake in small tube pan in 350 degree oven until done.

## CORN MEAL DUMPLINGS
Cost, 10 cents (November 1941)
Serves 4 to 6   *Woman's Day Kitchen*

1    cup white corn meal
1    cup sifted flour
1    teaspoon baking powder
½    teaspoon soda
¾    teaspoon salt
1    tablespoon lard
1    egg, grade B
1    cup buttermilk

Sift dry ingredients together into a bowl; work in lard with fork. Combine well-beaten egg and buttermilk. Add to dry ingredients mixing only enough to moisten flour. Do not mix until smooth. Drop by teaspoonfuls into gently boiling pot, broth, soup, or on top of turnip, mustard or collard greens. Cover, cook 20 minutes. Serve at once.

## SHAMPOO
Flake a bar of castile soap. Melt soap in one pint of boiling water, then cool. Put soap mixture into mixing bowl, and add one egg. Beat with rotary egg beater; put in jar. After it settles, it is ready to

use. This shampoo will keep indefinitely.

Reva Seckington
Marshall, Missouri

## Homemade Grape Nuts

We were poor (didn't know it at the time), and I'm of a large family, oldest daughter of a family of six girls and five boys. We didn't buy boxed cereal, we used oatmeal and mother would grind up the leftover biscuits, put them in the oven and brown them good. They were kind of like Grape Nuts cereal - and a sprinkle of cinnamon helped. We made our own kraut (sauerkraut), hominy, lye soap. To get the *Capper's Weekly* we usually traded a few old hens for it.

Dessie Pinkley
Elkland, Missouri

## Mom Was Best Bread Baker

Growing up we ate lots of rice and raisins cooked together. We then added cinnamon, sugar and cream, and was it ever good. My mother always had "home-made" cinnamon rolls to go with it. Lots of times that was our whole meal. Our mom was the best bread baker in the county. She baked every other day for years, for there was 11 that sat down for a meal. Lots of fried potatoes found their way to the table. A favorite meal was fried potatoes served with mustard sardines. We also broke up bread, scrambled a few eggs over and fried it in a little butter. Another favorite was to cook macaroni, then scramble a few eggs and pour over and fry this. We also ate a lot of pinto beans and fried bread dough. To make these, make your bread dough. Heat some oil in a skillet. Cut off small pieces of the dough and drop it in the hot oil. Brown and then turn and brown the other side and drain on paper towels.

Mildred O. Waldren
Tribune, Kansas

## Natural Provisions

Memories of the Great Depression are etched deeply and permanently in my mind. These were bittersweet days, testing the mettle of people living at that time, as they sought ways to survive. And we did survive by faith, courage and ingenuity.

During the spring and summers, people who had gardens carried water from struggling wells to thirsty rows of vegetables.

If fruit trees and roadside vines and berry bushes produced, neighbor women and children gathered wild plums, wild grapes, elderberries, currants and gooseberries. Chiggers, heat and dust were forgotten when gleaming jars of fruit and shimmering glasses of jellies, jams and preserves sparkled on pantry shelves.

Although it would appear that, with such provisions, the depression was not so severe, these products of the land were not all available as they competed against insects, birds, wind and drought. But we learned to gather all we could to preserve. Nothing was wasted.

We enjoyed the bounties as plates of rich, red tomato slices came to our table, along with green beans cooked with sautéed onion, and crisp bacon pieces. Bowls of fluffy mashed potatoes, creamed peas, glazed carrots, buttered corn or roasting ears brightened our meal-times, one vegetable at a time, usually never more than two at one meal. Gravies, cream style or flavored with homegrown meat products, often accompanied the potato dishes and helped to stretch the food supply.

Flocks of chickens were fed on home-grown grain. Each spring most farm families ordered strong crates of young chicks, which were housed and fed, until roosters reached frying size. It was then that platters of crispy fried chicken graced the table. Others were canned in glass jars and allowed to cook slowly at low heat. We knew these would be a part of our winter meat supply.

A few hogs were kept in a pen near a grain and water supply, where excess milk, mixed with ground corn or other grain, could be poured into long wooden troughs for their use. Hogs also found potato and apple peels and discarded fruit a delicacy. At a certain weight, a hog was butchered. Bacon and hams were sugar-cured or preserved in a salt-water brine. This brine was prepared in a wooden barrel, and deemed strong enough to preserve the hams, bacon, tenderloin and sausage when the salt content was strong enough that an egg would float on the surface of the brine.

When the grain had been harvested and threshed, we loaded a trailer with a certain number of bushels of wheat and took it to the mill in Abilene, Kansas, where it was weighed and graded. The wheat was then traded, its value computed against the value of 50-pound bags of flour, which we stored in large lard cans until my mother turned it into crusty loaves of bread, cinnamon rolls, biscuits, pancakes, and the delicious **Eggless Cake** she made if the eggs had been sold. The following is her recipe:

1   cup sour milk
1   cup sugar
2   cups flour
½   cup shortening
¼   tsp. salt
1   tsp. baking powder
½   tsp. baking soda
1   tsp. cinnamon
1   tsp. allspice
1   tsp. nutmeg

Cream sugar and shortening. Sift flour, measure and sift with baking soda, baking powder, salt and spices. Add alternately with milk to first mixture. Beat thoroughly. Pour into well-oiled loaf pan. Bake in moderate oven (375 degrees) for 45 to 50 minutes. (This recipe was taken from the old Searchlight Cookbook, published by *Capper's* in the depression years and was submitted by Mrs. F. M. Crasse of Logan, Iowa.) This was one of our depression day desserts we enjoyed so much.

Reva M. Smith
Abilene, Kansas

## Karo Syrup Sweetener

Depression days were sad, happy, and also hectic, yet most of us came out of them with a better understanding and compassion for people.

I believe that one of the hardest parts of the depression was not being able to buy some of the little treats we wanted.

To help us satisfy our sweet tooth we had a favorite cookie recipe. We used our favorite sugar cookie recipe, then we substituted one cup of Karo syrup plus two tablespoons of sugar for each cup of sugar. It didn't matter if it was dark or light, they still tasted good and Karo syrup was cheaper.

Meat wasn't too plentiful and we made what I called the end of the garden stew. By taking some of all the vegetables I had in the garden, I boiled them in lightly salted water with one fourth cup of butter or oleo. When tender I thickened them with a milk thickening. When served with baking powder biscuits it was delicious and filling.

Evelyn Williams-Hall<br>Sioux City, Iowa

## New Year's Cookies

I was a preschooler at the start of the depression years so was not really aware of all the difficulties my parent undoubtedly had providing necessities. One instance I vividly recall was when a neighbor lady lost her husband and was left with five small children. Our family had gone over to help her and she invited us to stay for the evening meal. The kitchen had a long table with backless benches on either side. All we had for supper was homemade bread with lard spread on it. I remarked not liking lard but the nudge of an elbow signaled for me to be quiet and eat. Even though a meal at home might be homemade bread and fruit, we had butter to spread on it as we generally had a cow. Daddy would sell milk for 10¢ a quart after reserving enough milk so Mama would have cream to make butter.

New Year's Day was special because of the custom where I

grew up of making what were called New Year's Cookies. The smell of them cooking and then waiting for them to cool enough so we could dunk them in sugar seemingly always took too long. Here is Mother's recipe she used, just as she had it written in her well-worn notepad which served as a recipe book.

NEW YEAR'S COOKIES

1  cup cream
1  cake yeast
3/4  cup sugar
2  cups milk
4  eggs
3  cups raisins
1/2  tsp. salt
5  cups flour

Heat milk to little more than lukewarm. Add yeast, cream, salt and sugar. Beat eggs well, add raisins and enough flour to make soft dough. Let rise until double in size. Drop into hot fat by the spoonful and fry to a golden brown.

> Mabel Nyland
> Norton, Kansas

## Last Of Garden Vegetables

This old recipe is cheap and tastes good, and looks colorful. I still enjoy doing this recipe with the last of garden vegetables. I use turkey bacon and Puritan oil instead of bacon and bacon grease. Sometimes I serve this dish with cornbread.

Use 10-inch iron skillet.

Fry bacon. Drain. Save for later.

Fry chopped onion in bacon grease until translucent.

Then add and continue to fry:

Chopped green Bell peppers

Sliced potatoes that have been boiled.

Cut up, chopped, red tomatoes (you can use canned tomatoes, tomatoes are the main ingredient)

Then, crumble the saved, drained bacon on top of the rest of the vegetables. Season with salt and pepper to taste. Season with

1 teaspoon chili powder. (Or cut up hot peppers.)
Stir and simmer these ingredients together.
Cook, covered, on low heat for 15 minutes.
Serve with bread and butter and iced tea.
Heat leftovers (can be frozen) and serve with scrambled eggs.
You can make a large or small amount depending on how many vegetables you have.

> Naomi J. Ochs
> Independence, Missouri

## Sweet Revenge

We sold cream to buy our groceries, and it seemed that all the store carried was oatmeal. I have just gotten to where I can stand the sight of it in the last few years. I'm not overly fond of mutton, either, after eating potatoes fried in mutton tallow for weeks on end, until we could afford lard again.

It was customary for the grocer to include a sack of candy with each bill of groceries purchased. Since there were six children in our family, we all made sure that we got our fair share. I was the only boy at home, and on occasion, my sisters would tease me unmercifully. However, I had ways to get revenge! When the candy was divided, I would make a pretense of eating all of mine, but would manage to save at least half of it. When the teasing became too much, I would slip off, go to where I had hidden the candy, get a piece of it, and then, about ten minutes later, stand in fron of the girls and s-l-o-w-l-y eat the candy. In this case, revenge was truly sweet!

> Rollie L. Campbell
> Ignacio, Colorado

## Food Seemed To Vanish

We didn't have much of a variety of food to eat during the winter. Mama made large dishpans full of hominy which she would cook different ways. We always had lots of cottage cheese, home-baked bread and beans. Dad would buy peanut butter in five-pound cans and Karo syrup by the gallon buckets. When he would get some of the hay sold he would buy gunny sacks full of Irish potatoes. But with that many mouths to feed, food just seemed to vanish.

In the summer time we picked bushels of sand plums and wild grapes, but Mama didn't have sugar to make jelly and when she had sugar there was no such thing as Sure Jell or Pen Jell so her jelly turned out like syrup.

I have a cookbook that I made during the Depression.

### CHOCOLATE CAKE

    2   eggs
    ½   cup shortening
    1   cup molasses
    2½  cup flour
    ¾   cup cocoa
    ½   tsp. salt
    2   tsp. soda
    1   cup hot water

Beat eggs, add melted shortening, molasses and mix well. Sift dry ingredients together, add alternately with water. Bake in two nine inch greased layer pans at 350 oven for 30 minutes. Spread with Depression frosting.

### FROSTING

    ½   cup flour
    3   Tbsp. cocoa
    ½   cup sugar
    Pinch of salt
    Sweet Cream to moisten.

Sift flour, cocoa, sugar and salt together, add cream gradually, stirring constantly until icing is of right consistency to spread. Beat hard until smooth. May add 2 Tbsp. orange juice.

Mildred Parker<br>Atkinson, Nebraska

## Popcorn A Treat

For popcorn balls we'd put on canvas gloves and rotate an ear of popcorn in our hands 'til the kernels fell off. Then a fire would be built in the iron woodstove and the corn popper brought out. When the stove lids were hot, the square screen box of the popper was filled with kernels and with the long handle of the popper we pushed it back and forth on those hot lids 'til the box was filled with popped corn. This was emptied into a big bowl and we'd start over again 'til we had enough for a few dozen popcorn balls.

The kitchen had tall cabinets reaching to the ceiling. At one end of the countertop a bin opened at an angle to hold a 100 lb. sack of flour. You can see that people baked a lot in those days. Mother baked eight loaves of bread every Saturday. Should we happen to run out of bread for Saturday lunch she would pinch off a piece of fresh dough, shape it into a patty and fry in a pan. These were positively delicious when cut open and spread with butter and jam. Today one might call them English muffins.

There were no restaurants or fast food eating places. One might have dinner at the hotel in town. Sometimes before or after a movie we would have an ice cream at the ice cream parlor.

Irene Duddy<br>Tucson, Arizona

## "Bare Bones"

I have never understood how our neighborhood grocer managed to carry the credit accounts for the many families like ours who were existing for days and sometimes weeks before being able to pay their accounts. Mom was great at making meals out of "bare bones" - almost, anyhow. My favorite noon meal on school days consisted of soup beans flavored with a hambone accompanied with bread or oleo (or butter on rare occasions). Sunday dinners were often built around roast beef tongue or perhaps roast beef heart. Chicken was an occasional delicacy.

When my brother-in-law and sister butchered (usually a hog or two) on their farm, Dad and Mom helped them. They always shared meat with us. Not much of the hog went to waste. The pig's knuckles were pickled. The ears and some of the head meat were made into "souse." Head "cheese" was also made from cooked trimmings from the head of the hog. There was also a mixture of cornmeal and head meat that was cooked like corn meal is, in making mush. After it was chilled and solid, it was sliced and eaten fried just like mush. At home it was called "pawnhaas." I'm not sure of that spelling, but at least that was the way it was pronounced. There were "cracklings" left from pressing the liquid lard out of the cooked fat trimmings of the hog. They were good and rich to the taste, but the tummy could not handle too much of them.

Marvin E. Hanson
Boone, Iowa

## Monotonous Diet

At times our diet got monotonous, but we were never as bad as some we knew. People with lots of turnips and not much else tried fixing them every way, even turnip kraut.

We bought no meat except canned salmon. It could be fixed so many ways to stretch for ten. We ate it made into soup made with milk, or made into fish cakes, and my sis made lots of it into a baked escalloped salmon dish. We also bought canned corn and it was made into soup with crackers. We churned our own butter and I often took a turn at cranking the old daisy churn. We had biscuits every morning, and took them as sandwiches in our school lunches at first. No one used bakery bread then. We ate cornbread or whole wheat bread baked like cornbread, often the grains were taken to the mill at town for the cornmeal and graham flour. If we ran out of it mother baked white flour "batter bread" for supper. It was cut out like cornbread, too, what is called "spoon bread" in the south.

Jewell Cooper
Bolivar, Missouri

## Simple Fare

My father talks about how his family would eat the potato peelings at one meal and the potatoes at the next meal to keep from going hungry.

They collected dandelion greens to eat. They had a vegetable garden and fruit trees.

Here are some recipes:

### GREEN TOMATO MINCEMEAT

| | |
|---|---|
| 1 | peck green tomatoes (cut up) |
| 5 | pounds brown sugar |
| 2 | tablespoons salt |
| 2 | tablespoons ground cloves |
| 2 | tablespoons cinnamon |
| 2 | tablespoons allspice |
| 1 | cup vinegar |

Bring to a boil.

Add:

| | |
|---|---|
| 1 | pound raisins |
| 1 | pound currants |
| ½ | peck apples (cut up) |

Cook until thick.

Put into canning jars and seal.

### MOLASSES COOKIES

| | |
|---|---|
| 1 | cup molasses |
| ½ | cup soft shortening |
| 2½ | cups flour |
| 1¾ | teaspoons baking powder |
| 1 | teaspoon salt |
| 1½ | teaspoons ginger |

Allow dough to stand at room temperature 20 - 30 minutes. Roll out very thin. Cut rounds with floured cutter. Bake about 7 minutes at 350 degrees.

### ONE EGG CAKE

Combine:

| | |
|---|---|
| ½ | cup butter |
| 1 | cup sugar |
| 1 | egg |

2    cups flour (sifted)
1    cup milk
1    teaspoon vanilla
Pinch of salt
2 teaspoons baking powder
Bake at 350 degrees for 30 minutes or until sides pull away from edge of pan.

Meredith Sorenson
Fairport, New York

## Jelly From A Chicken?

Red Hen Jelly was a store-bought spread that we ate reluctantly, only after exhausting our winter store of home-made preserves. I hated this sorry excuse for jelly. Pale pink in color, flavorless, with the consistency of rubber, it came in a "tin" pail which was probably more desirable than its contents, The jelly must have been pure pectin with a drop or two of food coloring. The pail was readily identified by a red hen on the label. I couldn't help wondering how they made jelly from a chicken, red or any other color.

Myrna Kautz
Merrill, Wisconsin

## Succulent Shoe Box Recipes

I have a scrapbook on Depression days stories, clippings, pictures, etc. I am the 8th child of 12, my parents were married 66 years. Ours was and still is a loving family. Here is Mama's recipe for Depression days cake (eggless):

1    cup white sugar
½    cup milk
1    cup flour
1    teaspoon baking powder
1    cup uncooked raisins
Method: Make a batter with above ingredients, pour mixture in an 8 x 8 oiled pan. In a saucepan combine these ingredients; 1 cup

brown sugar, 1 tablespoon butter, 2 cups of boiling water. Cook over medium heat until sugar dissolves, then add 1 teaspoon vanilla. Pour this hot mixture over the cake mixture and bake 25 minutes in a 350 degree oven. Serve warm.

This cake was served often in our home - Mom would often make one cake for dinner and another one for supper. During World War II days syrup or sorghum was substituted in place of rationed sugar. Still was good.

My mama left her dog-eared, yellowed recipes, collected in an old shoe box tucked away down in the kitchen cabinets, a legacy to her "Memory Hungry" grown children. Of course this recipe was tripled during her cooking days, so I have tried to cut it down to 1992 times.

Mary Lu Beemer Schofield
Lenox, Iowa

## Castoria

Here is my recipe for the way I made Castoria for us.

2 oz. Senna leaves

2 oz. rochell salts

5 cent oil of winter green

Boil leaves in 1 quart of water and boil down to 1 pint.

Strengthen boil with 2 cups of granulated sugar.

Add salts, remove from stove and add wintergreen. Cool and bottle.

Alice Jenkins
Lamoni, Iowa

## Family Recipe

### BAKED BEANS

Boil one pound large dried limas in salt water.

In frying pan cut about 3/4 lb. bacon and fry. Add 1 cup onion.

Don't throw bacon fat away unless it's too much.

Add 1 regular can tomatoes.

    1   can of tomato soup

1 cup dark Karo syrup
¼ cup dark brown sugar
Salt and pepper to taste.
Add to cooked, drained limas in a large casserole. Bake about 1½ hours at 350 degrees.

Helen Jacobs
Clarence, Missouri

## Peanut Patties

Made from peanuts and syrup or sugar. Parch the peanuts, then shell them. Measure your syrup or sugar. Cook until it turns to a syrup (thick bubbling). Then butter your pan or platter. Pour your bubbling thick syrup into your buttered pan or platter. Let it stand until cool. Then cut into squares.

We would select a number two or three wash pot. We would put two gallons of corn and an eight pound bucket of ashes into the wash pot. The ashes were made by burning oak limbs around the pot. Then we poured in enough water to cover the corn. We then built a fire around the pot and cooked the corn until it was tender. Then dipped out of the pot, washed well until free of ashes. Now it was ready to be carried to the kitchens to be served.

Willie Mae Faulkner
Shreveport, Louisiana

## A Depression Christmas Dinner

Mother's parents came from England on their wedding trip in 1873. The English are not noted for being excellent cooks, and maybe my mother was not an outstanding cook, but she had learned her lessons well from her English mother.

During the Depression we had chicken for Christmas dinner. Of course, it was boiled, not roasted. With it my mother served the very best baking powder biscuits drowned in the gravy made from the water in which the chicken had been boiled.

She served mashed potatoes and mashed boiled rutabagas. Being English, we poured vinegar over our rutabagas.

Usually there was cabbage salad. This was made with

shredded cabbage molded in lemon jello.

There were home-canned beet pickles and dill pickles.

The highlight of the meal, of course, was the eagerly awaited Plum Pudding.  The recipe had been brought to America by my grandparents.  The sauce was a simple one made with brown sugar and water, thickened with cornstarch and flavored with lemon extract.

Later in the afternoon we shelled mixed nuts with a nutcracker and dipped each nut-meat in salt – enough to make sodium-conscious people shudder.  For those who had regained their appetites therre were shiny red apples.

Mary Gaylord
Balsam Lake, Wisconsin

## Good Ole Days

Depression days in Oklahoma
A time when cash was rare,
A homemade lunch to carry
But we really didn't care.
No store-bought box had we
To hold our meager fare

Of biscuits holding fried eggs
Or home-grown slabs of meat,
Perhaps a baked potato -
Either Irish, white, or sweet.
In fall there'd be an apple
Which was a special treat.

A lard bucket or syrup pail
Would hold whate'er we took
To feed ourselves at noontime
Break from poring over our books.
"What's in your lunch today?
Mind if I take a look?"

# HEARTY FARE

Warm days we ate outdoors
Clustered with our pals.
Grassy plots or on the stile
Were favorites of the gals.

Some carried milk in a jar,
A thermos was unknown.
Boiled eggs were often cracked
On a friend's noggin bone.
There were some schooldays
When lunch was bread alone.

We enjoyed what food we had
Never knowing we were poor.
Each day the lunch kept us
Until the farmhouse door.
We'd made it through another of
Those "good old days" of yore.

Nova Felkins Bailey
Beaverton, Oregon

# CHAPTER 3: Employment Opportunities

### Live On What You Earn

When I was growing up in the small farming community of Glasgow, Missouri, my parents didn't have a steady income. My dad did day work and also had a team and wagon for hauling. Eventually he bought a Model T truck. Some weeks he made several dollars, but would then go several days or weeks with little or no income. To help out, my mother took in boarders at the rate of $7.00 a week. We usually had two boarders in the house at any given time.

As soon as I was old enough, I worked at filling stations to help earn money for my folks. I hand-pumped gas from the old-type gas dispenser. I also washed and serviced cars. One time, while in high school, I worked at three filling stations at one time. I also had a *Kansas City Journal Post* newspaper route. Unfortunately, I had to give this up because many people could not afford to pay their subscriptions.

After high school graduation, I went to Moberly (Missouri) Junior College. As I played both football and basketball, the out-of-district tuition was waived. When I left home in early September I had $35.00 cash and an Austin automobile that I purchased for $65.00 (between semesters I had to sell the car. Fortunately I got my $65.00 out of it). In order to pay for college I worked in a bus station about four hours a day and eight to ten hours on Saturday and Sunday. I worked the counter and washed dishes in a restaurant for my food.

When I returned home from Moberly, I found out that my parents had several hundreds of dollars in delinquent bills, plus an $800.00 mortgage on the house. I would not be able to attend Southern Methodist University. I would have to find work and help pay the bills. I decided that in addition to paying off the debts, I would bring modern amenities into our home. On the top of my priority list were running water, an indoor bathroom and electricity.

I was able to get a job with the Army Corps of Engineers. My first job was working on the Missouri River unloading barges for 45¢ an hour. I was able to help pay off the debts and bring the modern amenities into our home. As I worked I began to advance and decided to stay with the Corps. I stayed with them for thirty-nine years.

Living through the Depression taught me to learn to live on what you earn, make the best out of what you have and save for the future.

Myrl E. Maddox
Cocoa Beach, Florida

## Remembering Parents' Courage

Recalling the events of the depression era, I have remembered most of all the courage of my parents. As a child, I accepted everything. As an adult, I realize not only how difficult the years must have been, but how resourceful people became in their struggle to provide for a family.

After his job on the railroad was eliminated, my father worked any job available. He raised chickens, planted a garden, cleaned school rooms, hauled garbage, shoveled snow, whatever the season required, he kept busy. He raised beautiful chickens and took good care of them. He remembered, from his working days on the railroad, the grain that remained on the floor of the box cars after they were unloaded. He asked, and received, permission to sweep up the grain, which he brought home for the chickens. He cooked peelings from the vegetables prepared for the family and fed those to the chickens. He gave names to several of his favorites. One particularly large white rooster was father's pet. He cradled him in his left arm on occasion, and brought him into the kitchen for a brief visit. They were fun to listen to as well. Dad spoke to him, as one would to a friend, and the rooster made little noises that seemed like a response. When the time came to sell chickens, he took them to our neighbor who owned a poultry business. He traded live chickens for dressed chickens. Needless to say, his pet rooster was not sold. We enjoyed our chicken dinners, knowing we were not eating "our friends."

Catherine Doyle
Fresno, California

## Town Farmers

We lived in the northeast Kansas town of Robinson, with a population of 300. Since our house was next to a pasture, we secured an easement to build a milking barn. We rented a pasture along Wolf River, which was four blocks from the barn. There were six cows which I took to the pasture of a morning and brought home after school. An old black jersey would let me ride her so she was always the last one out the gate where I would "mount up."

We had a milk route at night delivering pints, quarts or gallons to the residents. Whole milk was 25¢ a gallon. I rode on the running board of our '29 Chevrolet as my older sister, Ferne, drove the car. In the morning we delivered to one of the local grocery stores.

The milk was in glass bottles with waxed cardboard caps. In the winter, if the milk was left on the porch, as it froze it would push the cap up to as much as two inches of rich cream. Undelivered milk was put in stone crocks to be skimmed the next morning.

I recall having a date with my wife of 50 years. When I did not arrive at the barn on time, she came looking for me. I was in

Wolf River swimming a cow across that had gotten on the other side. I tease her about being a farm gal and she call me a "town farmer."

Walter R. Brant
Hiawatha, Kansas

## Dad's Resourcefulness

I was about nine years old when the economic collapse caused my Dad to lose his job as a moulder in the local grey iron foundry in our hometown of Auburn, Indiana.

Dad was too staunch a Republican to apply for a job with the New Deal's Public Works Administration. He felt it was too much like welfare and it was a Democratic ploy to buy votes! So he relied on his own resourcefulness in attempting to find work. His background as a farmer had given him many skills. I recall he picked up a couple of carpentry jobs. At one time he worked on a new dance hall being built north of town. Another job consisted of helping build a hip-roofed barn south of town. For a time he and a friend cut wood on the shares of some wooded acres owned by a farmer-relative.

Mom took in washing for several families who could afford such services. She also did housework for some of those families. In addition to the constant search for work we maintained not only a sizable garden on our property, but also planted vegetables in a large vacant lot just west of our home.

My mother's youngest brother was a traveling salesman. Somehow he managed to continue selling through those tough years, although he was forced to change products several times from his original position with Firestone. In his travels he came into possession of an electrical doughnut molding machine. Fashioned like a waffle maker, it contained six triangular molds into which cake doughnut dough could be poured. He gave the equipment to my parents, who were very willing to have a go at entrepreneurship.

Dad didn't take a fancy to selling. So he became the baker and Mom and I the sales force. I had a bit of experience selling

35

magazines earlier such as the *Delineator*, *Ladies' Home Journal* and *Saturday Evening Post*. Being in junior high I would go selling every evening after school and on Saturdays.

With the money I earned I was able to make installment payments to buy our family's first radio, a little Philco table model with a sort of cathedral shape to it. What a thrill! I no longer had to visit other friends' homes to listen to "Jack Armstrong the All American Boy," or "Little Orphan Annie" and all those other wonderful serial dramas.

Eventually Dad was called back to the foundry and his work as a moulder. However, the regular paychecks came too late to prevent the foreclosure by the bank on our house which my parents had started buying the year before my birth.

Marvin E. Hanson<br>
Boone, Iowa

## Welfare Delivers Goodies

Our bank closed on December 22, 1932. My brother-in-law had just taken a load of hogs to the Oscar Meyer company, and rushed to the bank with the check, and managed to deposit it just before the 2 p.m. deadline. Of course no one told him that he wouldn't get it back for a long, long time.

I had cashed my monthly teacher's check ($95) that day, but took it all in cash as I had some Christmas gifts to buy, and had signed up for life insurance and needed money for the first payment. That amounted to almost the only cash our family had on hand for a long time, so the insurance payment was delayed.

Since we lived on the farm, we always had plenty of food. A girlfriend of mine had gotten married that year, and just before her baby was born in November, her husband who had worked at Rock Island Harmester Co., got laid off, so we went to visit them and brought them some potatoes. We could only sell the large potatoes, so those we gave away were the smaller ones, like those we ate. We also took some canned fruit to them. Her husband, who just laid on the cot all afternoon, made fun of the small potatoes. While we were there, Welfare delivered their free groceries, which contained oranges, lettuce and all other things that we could not afford to buy at the stores. That man never did hold a steady job again...said, "Why should I?"

Name Witheld
Davenport, Iowa

## Employment Variety

I was quite young at the time of the great Depression, being born in 1921 and only 7 years old at the time of the market crash in 1928.

My father had been a successful farmer up to the time of my birth, when through an unfortunate accident he had to give up farming.

Three rooms of the second floor were rented out for income. One family of four came to rent the rooms for some time. The father rolled cigars and then delivered boxed cigars to sell to the nearby small towns.

The side lot next to the house was made up into a kitchen garden. Here were grown lettuce, tomatoes, radish and vegetables. The neighbor ladies came to buy a sprig of dill for their pickling of cucumbers. My sister and I would sell a sprig for a nickel and then run to the neighborhood grocery store for a store-bought candy bar.

My brother had a daily paper route and also delivered Reminders for the local merchants. In 1931 he saved enough money to buy our first radio. He also saved cancelled stamps and sent them away to receive new stamps. Postcards were a penny then and a letter could be mailed for a three cent postage stamp.

I was 13 years old when we moved to the Twin Cities in 1934. That year my older brother qualified for a government job through taking a Civil Service examination. He went to work for the large sum of $100 a month. Franklin D. Roosevelt was President. Government jobs were the salvation of some of the problems of the time. I, myself, took a summer nursemaid job for $3.50/week. I worked 11 a.m. to 6 p.m. Monday through Friday. The money I earned that summer paid for my class ring and prom dress for graduation in 1939.

After graduation I went to work for Montgomery Ward and Co. as a salesgirl for 35¢ an hour. But my co-workers and I went out to lunch once a week, payday. A good lunch cost only 35¢.

Irene Duddy
Tucson, Arizona

## Early Grocery Store

Sometimes as I shop for groceries in a large supermarket, I think back many, many years ago. Almost 50 in fact! I worked as a clerk in a large (for Mayetta) grocery store. Mr. Jones was the owner, I was the only hired clerk, and together we would wait on seventy-five to one hundred families every Saturday night after the free picture show. We wrote each order down and got all the cans and supplies ourselves as the customer read off his or her list. No one thought of waiting on themselves as they do today. We had a cash register, but the only thing it was used for was keeping cash in. There was no way it would add up an order or tell you what change to give like the ones today. You did that in your head.

Very few wrote checks as most everyone paid with cash. I wonder now if the people who ring up your groceries would even know how to make change by themselves.

During the war we sold coffee, sugar, and even shoes. The only dry breakfast food in a box was Post Toasties, but not many of them were sold. Folks ate bacon, eggs, oatmeal, etc., for breakfast back then. We even took in eggs as cash. The eggs had to be counted and when folks had thirty dozen, that took some time! It was hard to keep one's mind on dozens of eggs when you were making change, taking rationing coupons, checking availability, and writing down the orders.

But I loved it. As the clerk I did the sweeping, dusting, keeping the windows clean, and I often put coal in the large stove that warmed the store.

I never thought I would see dog food, diapers, firewood, toilet paper and paper towels in a grocery store. Or the machines that tell customers what they have bought as the order is added up. I worked from 7 a.m. to sometimes 10:30 p.m. All this for $10.00 a week!

Alice R. Wamego
Holton, Kansas

## Turnips For Ten Hours

My family came to Tulsa from a Missouri rented farm in 1927. Calvin Coolidge was President. There were seven children, and my dad walked the streets looking for work. The only place he could find work was for some farmers in the south end of Tulsa. They wouldn't pay any money, but for ten hours of work they would give him two bushels of turnips, or occasionally two bushels of sweet potatoes. There is no way to eat a turnip that hasn't been tried by my family.

My Dad finally went to work on a rich man's estate, push-mowing eight acres of lawn, plus any other work, and milking their cow. He was so grateful for this $60.00 a month job that he stayed there 28 years, until he retired in 1961, when he was paid $200.00 a month.

Hollis Kelsey
Henryetta, Oklahoma

## Buster

I was a teenager during the depression years, but I remember them with fondness. My father owned and operated one of the first IGA grocery stores, and it was an interesting experience to get people to help themselves to the groceries on the open shelves. Many customers gave us their list of groceries and we had to gather the items from the shelves.

Our family had a black and white Shetland pony named Buster who did a lot of work cultivating a huge garden and truck patch. He also gave us a lot of pleasure taking us to the swimming hole at the dam or to Stone Lake to go fishing. He was also the means for me and my brothers to earn money. We took the seat off the buggy and made a wagon with which we hauled piles of ashes for people around town at ten cents per load. The town dump where we hauled the ashes and the trash is now the site of a large lumber yard, among other businesses. One Saturday job was hauling ashes for the local bakery, which paid fifty cents and kept us in spending money for five cent ice cream cones and ten cent hamburgers. You could even buy many things at the candy counter for one cent in those days!

Lotus E. Troyer<br/>Chenoa, Illinois

## Good Wage Shortage

Good jobs were very difficult to find. Even if work was exchanged for necessities, still it seemed the value received for work done was short due to the economy of the times.

An employer was hard-pressed to pay a good wage at this time, even for an excellent worker. Farm hands in a western section of Kansas reported they received 15¢ a day, plus board, room and laundry. Some, would work, for an allotment of meat or vegetables if an employer had enough.

Some men out of work wandered the dusty roads, laboring for food and shelter for a day, a week, or for however long they were needed. Neighbors traded work to save what money they had, men helped each other with farm work and women assisted each other with gardening, food preservation, making clothing and quilts for winter.

Reva M. Smith<br/>Abilene, Kansas

## Worked Their Way Through

My mother never failed to bake a birthday cake for whoever was having a birthday. Never a gift, but always a cake - except once. We had taken a trip to Arkansas. My brother Everett had a pen pal there and they were going to get married. We were working our way thru to pay for gas and food. We had a tent and a little stove to cook on.  Going through Kansas we shocked wheat and oats for the farmers.  We had a friend and family there, too, that we wanted to visit.

When the job was finished we went to Arkansas and picked grapes for awhile to earn some money.  Then we drove on to Lost Corner, Arkansas, northeast of Russellville, where my brother's pen pal lived.  We spent a week there and Everett and Iva got married.

Once more we were out of money so Everett sold his car and had money enough to get to Oklahoma where we stopped to pick cotton.  None of us had ever even seen any.  We had to buy each a sack to pick in, which just about put us out of money again!

Hazel Caruthers
Burlington, Kansas

## Thought She Had It Made

I graduated from high school in 1937.  For a few months I did housework for $3.00 a week plus room and board.  Then I got a jopb as a clerk in a small bakery for $10.00 a week.  I supported myself on that $10.00 a week.  Then it was a job at Northwestern Bell Telephone for $75.00 a month, and I really thought I had it made!

Ruth DeBuse
Omaha, Nebraska

## Barber Shop Blues

Pappa owned a barber shop.  Once, it had been a booming business, where every customer had his own shaving brush and named mug lined up on shelves before a mirrored wall.  The lovely odor of bay rum after-shave always made me close my eyes and breathe deeply whenever I entered.  But now, most men had to shave themselves and some wives had learned to cut the family's hair.  I didn't know why my mother often had a silent, pinched look about her mouth.  Then one day she left the Account Book open.  I could read and saw the total of the previous week's earnings - $9.25! Little wonder I saw her mending and re-mending her corset and just about everything else.

"Waste not, want not!" she would sing out. "Good thing I can sew!" Mamma was dauntless, putting on a good front for all of us most of the time.

Jean Carpenter Welborn
Tucson, Arizona

## Dad Was A Butcher

We had a CCC camp here for young homeless men. They were paid a very small wage, and provided room and board. They spent their time cutting brush, and building the WPA "White Houses" (outdoor toilets which were a big improvement over what the people had been using).

Dad was a butcher by trade. He bought fat cattle from the farmers, and contracted a sale to a grocery meat market. When evening came he would go to the country and kill the beef or hog, bring it home, skin it, string it up between two trees, wash it down good and let it cool out. Early next morning it would be taken to the store. He made cuts into steaks, roasts, and hamburgers, too.

Jerry Tudgay
Osage City, Kansas

## Seven Cents To Spend

My father had a job herding sheep that paid $25.00 a month. Our family of eleven existed on that and jobs us children could get working in the fields during the summer and fall.

The year I was sixteen I had seven cents to spend the first six months of the year. I bought a three cent stamp and four post cards. (Postage for letters was three cents and one cent for cards.) I sent for free samples of cosmetics and cookbooks for myself and the girls in my home economics class.

Our parents owned a small farm, a few horse, cattle and

chickens. Even tho we didn't have enough to eat or adequate clothing we thought we were better off than those people who traveled around and lived in covered wagons and sold crepe paper flowers.

> Jeneal Riley
> Rogers, Arkansas

## Low-Interest Lending

My wife is my age, and consequently relates her experiences from a different perspective. She attended Champaign High School where she learned typing. To become proficient, she advanced to Champaign Commercial College to better her skills. She had a job with the government in the Resettlement Administration until they moved to Indianapolis, which she refused to do. She typed many graduate college theses, which is an exciting job for the best of typists. She saved money, putting some into US Postal Savings at 2% interest, and removed it when the post office closed all those accounts out about 20 years ago. My first savings were in a band Savings Account, I was greatly disappointed when my small account paid only a few cents, which was at 3% interest. Banks were lending money at 6% - try to borrow for that today!

> Emmett Kirby
> Champaign, Illinois

## Well-Known Jobs

My father and uncle and many friends worked on jobs such as saw mills and pipelines. Day hands on a plantation got 50¢ a day. Other jobs were cutting hay, plowing, spreading gravel on the highway, cutting pulpwood, hauling logs with a log wagon, working on the railroad, and being a conductor on a passenger train. Fishing for a market, working at a dairy and well digging for drinking water were other well-known jobs.

> Willie Mae Faulkner
> Shreveport, Louisiana

## Depression Days

Imagine teaching a group of children from all grades during the Depression.

Days were long and work hard and pay poor – first 2 years $75 a month, then $69, then the last year $39 per month.

If kids didn't mind they would have to stand in the corner facing the wall, a punishment they didn't like so they behaved.

Teacher came early – to get in coal, start the stove, hang out the flag and bring in a pail of drinking water. Then it was time to ring the bell.

Many kids played tricks, but other kids would tell on them, so they had to stand in the corner, or miss recess or stay after school.

Helen Whitty
Webster City, Iowa

## A Dress Of A Different Size

Looking back to the '30s, I recall an incident which well could have ended my career in sewing if I had not turned about with a chuckle.

We had moved into a new neighborhood and a lady had asked if I could make her a dress. I had some experience in sewing so I volunteered.

This happened the third time my husband came home to find me sweating and tearfully struggling to make this dress fit the lady, who insisted it just didn't fit right.

I remember my husband took the dress, threw it across a chair and said, "Now listen, the next time that old "gal" comes back for a fitting, you tell her she's trying to get you to do something you can't possibly do." Innocently, I inquired, and he said, "Yes, she wants you to make a size that you can wear to fit her and that's impossible!"

Verna Sparks
DeSoto, Missouri

# CHAPTER 4: The Way Things Were

## Our Private Telephone

The telephone of my childhood in the 1930s was mounted on the dining room wall of our farmhouse. By today's standards it would be considered an antique. Encased in a rectangular shaped lacquered box, it appeared almost life-like with its two round bells for eyes and a long adjustable snout that became the mouthpiece. Below that was a small hinged shelf.

It was the exact replica of the ones in the homes along the party line. There was one big difference, ours was a private line!

It was so private that no one could call us except Grandma. Because she lived alone, Dad knew it would give her a sense of security to be able to contact us whenever she wished.

Since we were a mile away from the community telephone line, Dad ran a wire from our house to the barbed wire fence that formed the boundaries of our land and joined that of the home place where Grandma lived. On the other end he ran a wire into Grandma's house and attached it to her phone.

Grandma was on the party line so Dad installed a lever-switch. When the lever was up on her phone she was attached to the party line. When the lever was pulled down her phone was connected to the barbed wire line.

Grandma kept in close contact, often relaying messages that she received for us. If we needed something that required the use of the outside line, Grandma placed the call for us. It wasn't as convenient as present day private lines, but served the purpose for which it was intended.

Juanita Urbach
Brush, Colorado

## First Aid - Depression Style

The playground of our one-room country school was alive with boys and girls, ages six through thirteen. It was recess and we stood in clusters watching the bigger boys who were teasing a billy goat that had strayed from the farmyard across the road. The boys got a thrill out of holding the goat by his horns while he wrestled and tried his best to get away from them. When at last he freed himself, he took after the closest one in sight.

"Look out, Juanita!" someone shouted, but the warning came too late. Before I knew what was happening, the billy hit me and I went sprawling to the ground. I was helped up, but I must have been a gruesome sight. The goat's horn had ripped the skin under my chin and left it hanging loose, dripping blood onto my clean dress.

The teacher came, took one look and sent for the lady across the road. They attempted to clean me up but were overwhelmed at the sight of the gaping wound. Not knowing what more to do, they folded a clean flour sack into a triangular sling, placed the wide part under my chin and knotted the ends on top of my head. "She'll have to have stitches," the neighbor lady said. And the teacher agreed.

My Uncle Ed, who was still going to school, was instructed to take me home on his horse. On the way we discussed doctors. I couldn't remember ever going to one and the thought of doing so was frightening. Stitches sounded like needles. I was afraid.

Mama was nearly hysterical when she saw me. I'm sure she thought her darling would never be the same.

Dad was more calm. He had grown up in a family of ten children and had seen similar sights. Drawing on old memories of how his mother dealt with emergencies, he came up with a solution.

He got a pan of warm water and a wash cloth. Gently, he sponged the blood away so he could survey the damage.

"Get me a raw egg," he said.

I'm sure Mama thought he was out of his mind, but she did as he said. He broke the egg into a dish and carefully peeled the inner skin away from the shell. Then he pulled the edges of my torn skin together and placed the thin, slimy membrane from the egg across the tear. As the egg skin dried, it drew my skin even tighter.

After giving the wound several days to heal, Dad soaked the egg skin off with warm water. Mama was surprised to see that I only had a thin hairline scar.

For a long time after that incident, brother and I insisted on egg skin bandages for all our minor cuts. We even went so far to brag to our playmates, "We don't go to the doctor, our Dad just patches us up with egg skin."

Juanita Urbach<br>Brush, Colorado

## Makeshift Jobs

My mother's father was a teacher in New York City when the Depression hit. The teachers agreed to cut their salaries in half so that all of them could continue to work. After the Depression, their salaries were never raised to where they had been before the Depression started.

My mother had a friend whose father committed suicide when he lost his job.

The next-door neighbor of my mother's family was an engineer. When he lost his job he sold apples on the street corner.

Mrs. Walker, the wife of the New York City mayor, started the Good Humor Ice Cream Company. She employed men who had lost their jobs.

Both my parents talk about only having ice cream on

birthdays and at no other times.

They also have said that during the Depression people only had to pay the taxes on their property. Mortgage payments were delayed.

My father's father had his own business during the Depression. People didn't pay their bills and my grandfather couldn't bring himself to send them a bill.

Meredith Sorenson
Fairport, New York

## Rural Life Less Stressful

This isn't just "My Folks' Depression Days," but most is of my own Depression days as I grew up in the Thirties.

Those years were hard. CCC Camps, WPA work, etc. helped us survive. Most people followed the motto, "Use it up; wear it out; make it do; or do without." Outgrown clothing was passed on to the next child or to neighbor children who could use it. Newspapers and magazines were shared. Anything needing repaired was patched, darned or mended. New articles of clothing were made from old.

Feed sacks and flour sacks were valuable. White sacks were bleached by boiling with lye until letterings came out. They were then used for sheets, pillow slips, tea towels, underwear, and handkerchiefs. I used ten-pound sugar sacks to make our boys' training pants. Printed sacks were used for dresses, blouses, children's overalls, curtains, and quilts. Heavy clothing was cut into blocks and made into comforters. Fabric scraps were used for quilts. Rags were torn into strips and then crocheted or woven into rugs.

Mothers gave their children hair cuts and often their husbands.

We saved waxed paper from cracker and cereal boxes and there weren't very many kinds of cereals. Sometimes a loaf of bread was bought and the wrapper was re-used.

One time I papered my pantry with newspapers - at least it was clean.

Beds had straw ticks. After threshing each year, clean straw was used to refill the ticks. A feather bed went on top of this.

Fuel was wood or coal. Lamps used kerosene. Telephones were on party lines. Each family had a different set of short and long rings as its call numbers. Farmers met occasionally to repair the telephone lines. The Operator at Central was a great help in relaying messages. Some enjoyed eavesdropping to hear the news.

We had a country doctor everyone loved and he kept busy. We also used home remedies such as salt water to gargle, or goose or skunk grease rubbed on the chest with kerosene added (later much like Vicks was used). Alum cured mouth sores - how it puckered the mouth! A chicken feather swabbed the throat.

In today's lifestyle with so many toys, fast food places, clothes, TVs, videos, computers and all the modern conveniences, it sounds like life was hard then, and it was. We didn't realize we were so poor, as everyone we knew was in the same boat or worse. Life was less stressful here in the rural areas.

> Crista Taylor
> Livonia, Missouri

## Hitting Rock Bottom

The Nebraska Dust Bowl and Depression of the "Dirty Thirties" remains a vivid, painful memory to me. It continued all during my high school days. I came from a family trying desperately to save their farm. Every penny had to be clutched and saved. The town people were not affected as severely as the farmers as the continued drought compounded their miseries in a double way.

But I think the most painful memory was the day my Father lost one of his four remaining heifers. She had had her first calf and lost it, and died, too. We had endured dust storms for several days. Dad wore a wet cloth around his face. The choking stuff drifted into the house everywhere - on the window sills, into Mom's white curtains, across the floor. Outside it drifted over fence lines and machinery and it banged loose the barn doors. It literally blew the precious seeds out of the garden dirt, and that year a late frost had killed the buds on the fruit trees. So there would be no garden stuff or fruit to can and there'd be no potatoes to dig in the fall. And then the heifer died! Dad, my big, strong, gentle father, sat down on the front step and cried. Mom tried to comfort him but I ran and hid. I loved him so much! I have always wished that I would not have run away but stayed to help. We had all hit bottom that day.

And then things gradually began to get better. Dad managed to save the farm, and even helped his brother save his, too. The dust storms stopped, the rains came and President Roosevelt helped. We all survived!

Dorothy McClean Boettner<br>Fremont, Nebraska

## Time To Smell The Roses

As I reminisce about depression years these are the things I remember. My sister and I each had a "fancy" pair of stockings. All girls and ladies wore long stockings, we never dreamed of showing our legs in public. Well these fancy stockings had a kind a pattern woven and rayon and cotton knit threads of similar colors, but not the same. Our stockings were darned many times until each of us had one each that could not be mended anymore. Then the two "good" ones were given to me and I wore them to school. No one laughed as they were as poor as we were.

One of the things I did not like was the long underwear that bunched at my anklebone. We wore ankle-high laced shoes that never covered the bunch. I really never minded the four buckle overshoes - it helped to keep our legs warm, as you see there were no snowsuits and our gender never wore pants. Nothing was to suggest the shape of our legs! Girls began wearing day time pajamas in the mid 30s. Oh, times have changed.

Back in the olden days as well as the depression years almost everyone had a chicken house, a cow barn, fuel shed, and a large garden area, fruit trees, vines and bushes and don't forget winter onions and pieplant.

We did our own butchering of animals and chickens, ducks and geese. After a pig was slaughtered and cooled out by hanging on a tree branch, it was brought in before dark to be sure it was safe from 4-legged animals and 2-legged ones. Everyone was hungry. Meat, pork as well as beef, was quite often cut in small pieces and put in canning jars and then put in hot water and cooked for about 2 to 3 hours. We used the clothes boiler for our canner. When it had processed the proper length of time it was time to cool the jars and take them to the cellar or cave until used.

From pork the big slabs of fat were removed. The fat, too, was cut in small pieces or coarsely ground to render the fat into lard and cracklins. A cracklin is the cooked piece floating on top of the lard, and they were done when the cracklin had a dry sound when tapped by a spoon. Then the lard was drained off through a cloth in a colander. The lard was saved in canning jars or stone jars, with a board on top.

We had the dairy and delivered milk to people's houses in those glass bottles. We also had chickens, so with milk and eggs we made and froze our 6-quart freezer with ice cream every Sunday in warm weather.

Everyone remembers what they wish, but I do say the Depression will be remembered to me as "The Good Old Days." We did not have the strain of hurry, or were we concerned about keeping up with the Joneses. We enjoyed the simple things like star gazing. Back then "we had time to smell the roses!"

Dorothy Payne<br>
Ulysses, Nebraska

## Old-Fashioned Wash Day

Back on the farm, before the days of modern electrical appliances, Monday was wash day. Today we throw the dirty clothing in the washer and drier and call it doing the laundry, and it is done anytime the mood strikes us.

Back then wash day was a whole day's work and we went to bed tired and with a backache. Mother and I started that day by building a big fire under a huge iron kettle in the backyard at our farm home. The kettle was filled from a cistern of rain water that had drained from the roof of the house when it rained.

When the water became hot we filled the galvanized tub and added homemade soap to the water and inserted a wash board. The clothes were rubbed on the board to remove the dirt, then transferred to the kettle of water to which lye had been added. The clothing was boiled for about a half hour. We had an old broomhandle to punch the clothing as it boiled. While the white clothing boiled we washed the colored clothes and cotton dresses. Then came the real hard part: scrubbing dirty farm overalls that had collected their soil from the barnyard and fields.

Then the clothing was hung on a line in the yard to dry.

Marie Rea
Russellville, Missouri

## Beans, Bread and Laundry

Back in the good old days, in the 1930s, the #2 galvanized tub was as versatile and necessary in our house as a modern-day washing machine, shower and bathtub are today.

On wash day, as the boys brought their full buckets into the house, they emptied the water into the tub that had been put on the stove. There it would be heated for a future project. The tub would be about 2/3 full, and it would take some time for it to get hot enough to start the washing.

During that time Mom began sorting a batch of red beans by pouring them from one hand to the other, blowing on them to get out the smaller debris and picking out tiny rocks, dirt clods and other dregs until she was satisfied the beans were clean enough for our consumption. After rinsing them good, she poured cold water over them. Then she covered them with a lid and sat the big kettle on the back of the stove where it would stay the rest of the day, cooking slowly.

When she finished tending the beans, she began kneading down a batch of home-made light bread in the dishpan. At the right consistency, the bread dough was covered with a clean dish towel and set in a warm place behind the stove out of the draft.

Mom had three callouses on each hand from washing clothes all of those years. There was one on each "little" finger, one on each "ring" finger and one on the heel of each hand. They did not disappear until many years after she obtained an electric washing machine.

Mom also made her own starch. She began with a paste of flour and water to which she added boiling water. (No matter how hard she tried to get all of the lumps out, she always managed to leave one or two in, that invariably got stuck to one of my dresses, usually under one of the arms, or on my back where I couldn't reach.) When she felt the mixture was smooth enough she added cold water, thinning it to the proper consistency.

When the clothes were all tended to, she retrieved the dishpan full of bread dough from behind the stove where it had doubled in size. She greased the loaf-pans with bacon drippings, pinched a chunk of dough, shaped it, rolled it and laid it in the container, gently shaping it and smoothing it to fit the pan in which it would remain until it came out of the oven about 1½ hours later.

Eventually we all rallied around the table for a much deserved, hearty meal of hot light bread and freshly cooked beans.

Mary L. Hodson<br>Cornelius, Oregon

## Sales Brought Little Profit

During these depression years, products raised on the farm

in an amount available for sale brought little profit. Prices varied according to location, but in our area the prices paid for eggs at the purchasing center remained around the 12¢ a dozen level. Wheat produced during this time brought in the 25¢ a bushel range, which led many farmers to hold their wheat, grind it with other grains and feed it to their chickens and livestock, saving some for next year's planting.

A full gallon can of rich cream, taken to the local creamery, brought but $1.50 to $2.00. If one could sell the golden home-churned butter it would bring 35¢ per pound.

Local grocers sold milk from the nearby dairy for 11¢ to 14¢ a quart - or 7¢ - 8¢ if you had a bottle to exchange. Unsliced bread was sold for 5¢ -10¢ a loaf, or on very special sale days three loaves for 10¢ at our Cloverfarm store where a huge bunch of bananas hung on a hook from the rafters and one could buy a bag full for less than a dollar, if you had a dollar.

One hundred pounds of potatoes could be purchased for one dollar, if for some reason you had not raised any. Fifty pounds of beans cost $2.50. These were representative prices of staple items as they existed in our local area.

Reva M. Smith<br>Abilene, Kansas

## Maple Syrup Memories

When freezing and thawing days of February and March roll around, I am reminded of the activities on the farm at that time of the winter when I was a child. Nowadays to most folks it means snow, rain and fog one day and warm, sunny days the next, with a case or two of flu thrown in for good measure. But for those maple syrup makers this is the best time of all seasons. When the temperature is below freezing at night and the days warm up to around fifty degrees the sap flows fast in the maple trees, even before there is a hint of spring. About two weeks before, my father went into the woods of the Ozarks and cut pine trees just about the right size and hauled them down to the woodyard. There he cut them into two foot lengths and split them through the middle lengthwise, hollowed out the center of each half to make a trough in which to catch the maple sap. (Wooden buckets were too expensive.) Then he brought from the marshy places in the bottom field a load of box elder saplings and cut them in twelve inch lengths to be used as spouts. He heated a length of wire red-hot in the old fireplace and forced it through the entire length of each spout, forming a channel through which the sap could drain. One end of the spout was whittled down a bit for convenience at a later stage in the process.

When the sap was rising just right, my father hitched the team of horses to the farm sled and loaded in all the troughs, spouts, an augur, along with a hammer or two, and we headed for the maple sugar grove a half mile away. We drove through the grove, dropping off a trough at each tree until all were distributed, being very careful to keep the inside of each one as clean as a pin. A hole was bored into the tree about two feet from the ground and the small end of the spout driven into the hole. Imediately the rich, sweet sap began flowing through the spout dripping into the pine trough below. Two or three times a day we had to empty all this sap from the troughs into a barrel on the sled and store it until we had collected enough to fill the big boiler already set up over a dugout furnace in the side of the hill near the house. Huge piles of wood were ready to keep the fire roaring under the boiler the entire day, while the sap rolled and boiled, gradually turning a golden soft brown as the hours dragged by. The greenish white foam that boiled up every second must be skimmed off in order to improve the flavor of the finished product. The grown-ups took turns manning the skimmer, for it was a tiring task to stand there in the smoke and heat from the fire in front, while your back would be freezing. The skimmer was made by punching a dozen or so holes in the bottom of an old pie pan. This was to allow the juice to drain back into the boiler, and at the same time hold the "skimmings" in the pan to be dumped out on the ground. The pie pan was fastened to a long handle of a discarded broom so the tender could stand away from the hot, boiling sap to avoid getting scalded. It took forty gallons of sap to produce one gallon of syrup, so you see the greater portion boiled away and escaped as steam. It boiled vigorously until it was reduced to about two or three percent of the original volume.

Near the end of the day my father would begin testing every few minutes to see when it was the proper consistency for "stirring off." When it reached that stage the fire was pulled out from under the boiler and the syrup was allowed to cook a bit, then poured into various containers, properly covered, and stored away in the kitchen cupboard. The next morning for breakfast we would have country sausage with a big platter of fried eggs, hot biscuits and real butter doused with a plate full of maple syrup the likes of which we had not tasted since last year.

If you've been eating imitation-flavored maple syrup that comes from the grocer's shelf in a glass bottle, you're missing a delicacy that's never found outside a country kitchen close to a sugar maple grove.

Lola Garrett
Springfield, Missouri

## Milk On The Farm

Old folks do a lot of looking back to how it was when they were young. Life was not at all like it is today, and the difference affected the "well-to-do" along with the poor. City life was somewhat different from life out in the country even then.

You think of indoor plumbing and electricity. Well, city folks didn't have those luxuries either. They had coal oil lamps and outdoor toilets too, but they had one distinct advantage. Their milk was delivered to the door in glass bottles. The bottles had to be washed and returned but that was a small inconvenience. Out on the farm milk wasn't so easy to come by.

Every farm family had a milk cow. And she had to be milked twice a day come what may. At the crack of dawn and again at sundown somebody had to take a bucket to the cowpen and milk the cow. The cow usually had a calf in a small pen nearby and the calf was turned in with its mother to nurse enough to sustain it until the next milking time, then a little rope was put around the neck of the calf so he could be dragged unwillingly back to the pen. After that the cow was milked, making sure you got it all because the last part was where the cream was. Cream was churned into butter daily for the family table. There was no margarine in those days.

I've never understood why there wasn't more illness caused by such lack of sanitation. The cow had calf slobbers on her udders after the calf drank but it was ignored. It was important to milk the cow quickly while she had her milk let down.

Once to the house, the warm milk was strained though a cloth flour sack to hold back any trash that might have fallen off the cow while she was being milked, or any cowpen dirt that fell into the bucket when the cow tried to kick you.

The strainer cloth would be rinsed in cold water and pinned to the clothesline in the sun so it would be "clean" and ready to use at the next milking time. On Mondays this cloth was rubbed on the washboard and boiled with the white clothes in the big black wash pot in the back yard. Every woman saved soap grease to make her own lye soap for laundry and dishes as well.

Disposable milk filters were considered a great luxury when they became available. You could drink all of your milk then, instead of leaving the last bit in the glass because that was where the dirt settled.

When a farmer worked in the field until dark his wife usually milked the cow for him. Milking in the dark posed a problem because nobody had a flashlight back then. We had to light the kerosene lantern. Kerosene lanterns gave barely enough light to tell a cow pattie in the trail from a coiled up rattlesnake, but they sure beat nothing. They were used on the front porch for summertime visiting and were sometimes hung on the back of the wagon for a tail light when the family went to the annual nighttime school play.

On a blustery night in the springtime, light from the kerosene lantern led the way to the storm cellar, too. The only electricity was up among the clouds. Still, that way of life didn't seem so bad to us. Nobody had heard of the modern conveniences we have today.

Maxine Blackburn
Blanco, Texas

## Government Bought Stock

I graduated in 1930 from the eighth grade and lived on a farm until 1934 in the Mt. Zion School District. I lost my father when I was sixteen and had to take over the farm then. That was when the government shot and killed all the hogs and cattle in the depression. They gave the farmer ten dollars a head for cattle. This was in about 1933, when my father was still living. He refused to let the government kill any of his stock. My dad gave his bull calves away and sold his heifers to dairy farmers for fifty cents a head.

I stayed at home until I was twenty-two and then came to Watonga, Oklahoma, and farmed for my mother. We ate lots of black-eyed peas and made hamburger out of jackrabbits one winter.

T.R. "Tom" Johnson
Watonga, Oklahoma

## A Day to Remember

As near as I can recall it was a spring Saturday in 1933. Sometime after April, as I still had my birthday dime. It was because of the dime that I was going to town. It was tied in the corner of my handkerchief and nestled in my jacket pocket where I could feel it from time to time to make sure it was still there.

While Dad took in a sale, I was given permission to go uptown to spend my dime. Duckwall's was my destination.

I walked up and down each aisle, examining and pricing merchandise. There were rings, necklaces, bracelets, and fancy pins each priced ten cents. I eyed them carefully and went on to the make-up counter. Here I saw creams, lotions, lipsticks, rouge and Blue Waltz perfume. Further down were combs, barrettes, artificial flower corsages, scarves, etc. Most of these were within my price range.

Another counter was loaded with candy and gum. These sold from one to five cents. I looked at the paper dolls and leafed through the big little books also marked a nickel. I debated whether it would be better to buy two things or just one.

After my third or fourth time at the jewelry counter I asked to try on rings. I tried on several before I finally settled for a silver-colored setting with a bright blue stone. It fit perfectly.

Now that I no longer had money to spend I didn't feel welcome to be just "looking," so I retraced my steps along the opposite side of the street.

Juanita Urbach
Brush, Colorado

## Thank You, President Roosevelt

In 1929 at the very beginning of the Depression years my father moved us to Louisiana. I remember taking ½ dozen eggs to the store to trade for a tablet or pencils for school, perhaps I had a nickel left over for a candy bar.

We got seed loans which were paid back after the crop was harvested. Can were furnished by the Dept. of Agriculture for canning and sealers and pressure canners at central locations. Everyone brought their garden vegetables and helped each other can them for winter. These were enjoyable times for we could visit with our friends while working - many hands make light work.

I'm glad we experienced those days of working together and the simple pleasures we had. Thank God for President Roosevelt, who led the nation through the great depression and later World War II.

Lydia Jones
Medicine Lodge, Kansas

## Working For Water

We did not have any water on our land, and no electricity.  I remember how my Dad, with my brothers, would haul three big wooden barrels of water in a wagon a couple of times a week. He would hitch up a team of horses and go haul the water from the nearest spring, about five miles one way.  Dad had a Water Rig Drill Team come and twice they drilled over 300 feet down, but struck no water.  They even had a man called a "Water Witch" who would hold a forked branch from a tree, and this switch should pull down when he walked over a vein of water. It didn't work.

Barbara Parker
Agawam, Massachusetts

## The Biffy

The Biffy, better know as the Privy, was located about thirty yards from the back door of the dwelling.  The standard size of this building was large enough to accommodate two holes and was commonly called a "two holer."  Occasionally a deluxe model was available on the more pretentious farms as there was a third hole which was at a lower level for small children.

The setup was very tolerable in spring, summer and fall, but winter time was another story entirely.  The first path to be shoveled after a snowstorm was to the Biffy, and I must say that trips to that little house were made only because of extreme necessity, with no lingering or loitering thereabouts.

Summertime had its hazards also.  Several species of spiders had a tendency to seek out the dark recesses up under the seat. Probably ninety percent of these species were non-poisonous, but that did not contribute to one's feeling that the black widow spider might be hiding down there.

One amusing "spider" incident comes to mind and it happened as follows: my younger brother and I discovered a small hole on the outside just below seat level and large enough to accommodate a rather stiff pointed wire. One day we hid nearby and waited patiently until our older brother entered the Biffy. When we were certain he was seated comfortably, we sneaked up and stuck the wire through the hole, delivering a sufficiently hard jab with it. Such a commotion inside, and out he came, swearing he had been bitten by a spider. Of course we were laughing hysterically, which gave away what had actually happened and we all had a good laugh.

Indoor plumbing has all but eliminated the useful little building, and if I do occasionally see one in someone's backyard in the country, I wonder if it is still in use for its real intended purpose, or if it has been relegated by default to a spider factory.

Francis E. Hager
Phoenix, Arizona

## Rough Refrigerators

Many people who lived out in the country in the early thirties did not have electricity or gas. They did not have mechanical refrigerators or use ice boxes. The ice had to be shipped in on the train. A 100 lb. block of ice would be packed in sawdust and placed in a tow sack for shipping. Keeping fresh meat in the summer was a problem. In the summertime a farmer might kill a steer, divide it with his neighbors and take what was left over to town to sell. He would put the meat in a washtub shaded with a sweetgum limb to keep off the sun (and flies) and sell it from the back of his wagon. Housewives were anxious to get fresh meat so it had no time to spoil.

Containers of milk and butter were placed in pans of water. Fresh cool water from the well was drawn every hour or two. Bread and cake were placed in a pie safe - a cabinet with metal doors perforated in a design to allow air to circulate yet the food would be safe from mice or flies. The other food would usually be left in the cooking pots at dinner time, warmed up for supper and thrown out for dogs, hogs and chickens after the evening meal. There was no way to keep it from spoiling in the hot summer nights.

Eggs were fertile. No cook ever broke an egg directly into the mixing bowl. You tested it first in a saucer. There might be a baby chicken developing in the egg.

Margarine - oleomargarine - released thousands of acres of pasture land for other uses. Grazing land was needed to produce the nation's butter supply. Country families were slow to accept this new spread for hot biscuits. We were used to shortening in the store and this butter substitute was sold in a pound block and looked like shortening. You were required to mix the enclosed dry orange coloring yourself into the margarine until it became the color of butter. This took a little time and skill as often there would be a streak of orange that you hadn't blended in.

Gypsy Damaris Boston
Shreveport, Louisiana

## Hard Work By Hand

My father plowed the fields for corn planting with a plow that was pulled by the two horses we had. Everything was done this way as there were no tractors or machinery. Everything had to be done by hand. My brother and I would then plant the corn by walking from one end of the field dropping the grains of corn by hand in the rows. We would do this from early morning until dark. But we never seemed to mind, and we always felt we were lucky even though we had to work hard.

Etta Reiker
Union, Missouri

## Bank Closed – No Business

In the early '30s several companies went into bankruptcy. Banks were closed for two weeks. My folks took 60 dozen eggs to town to sell, but with the banks being closed, stores weren't even buying eggs.

Hogs were nine cents at market. Sold some and butchered some for their meat. But the worst part was the debt my folks owed.

Golda Erwin
McLeansboro, Illinois

## Bootlegging

During the depression of the early '30s, my father ran some poker games in our house. My father was a "meat carver," that is, he sliced the meat at a steam table in front of the customers. The slices of meat were so thin there was only one side to it! At least that was what was said, but the slices would hang over the side of the bread to such an extent it made the sandwich look larger than it really was. The bosses loved him because he was able to get his 200 sandwiches out of a round of beef. Most of the poker players were cronies he worked with; cooks, pastry cooks, chefs, bartenders, etc.

Dad would insist I go with him to his "bootlegger" to get the wine for his card players. During the Prohibition era, the Chicago Police Department was highly visible in its efforts to prevent crimes related to any of the violations of the 18th Amendment to wit: the Volsted Act. Automobiles in those days were still considered a "rich man's toy" to some extent. Laws were passed to detain any autos that had their shades lowered (takin' some guy for a ride) or, on the street after dark and suspicious looking. Therefore, an inconspicuous small car with a little boy in the front seat was definitely not very conspicuous. That was my dad's answer and we were never caught!

Bill Friar
Glen Ellyn, Illinois

## Tribute to Parents

Both of my parents were very hard-working people. Life

wasn't easy for them, but they never complained and seemed to enjoy life. However, when their children were big enough we all had our chores to do and it eased the burden on them.

They were very honest. They taught us to respect other people and most of all our elders. We were not allowed to call people by their first name. We said Uncle or Aunt or Mr. or Mrs. We were taught to never take anything that wasn't ours and to make sure you paid for anything you were buying and we were taught to tell the truth.

My parents were very hospitable. They never turned a bum away from our door without feeding him. It wasn't much sometimes, but my mother always gave them something.

Living on a farm in those days was a lot of work, but with parents like mine who never complained and were always doing their best, what child could ask for more? We never had a lot of material things, but we were given the rich heritage of being industrious, loving, kind, hospitable and honest.

Frances Duff Carter
Marquette Heights, Illinois

## Grandma's Apron

Grandma's aprons were not dainty things of beauty. They were truly "all purpose," made of dark colored calicos - mostly of dark blues, browns and dark greys (so the dirt wouldn't show!). Since her dresses were ankle length - so were the aprons. They were made of a straight piece of cloth gathered full onto a band that either buttoned or tied around the waist. Sometimes a square piece was stretched above the waist band to protect Grandma's dress up to the bust. The piece was usually pinned to the dress with safety pins.

There was always a pocket or two to hold her handkerchief, a bit of pencil, hairpins - anything small that couldn't be carried in the voluminous apron itself.

When Grandma went to the orchard she could pick up and carry - in her apron, of course - nearly a bushel of apples, peaches or pears.

With a quick flip of that apron she could "shoo" the old hens out of the flower bed or the vegetable garden.

Should a rainstorm come up quickly, Grandma could dash out and gather up a whole nest of baby chickens in that apron and get them to safety without any getting wet.

She carried lots of wood chips, corn cobs and kindling in that apron - to start fires in the old iron cookstove. Vegetables (peas, green beans, carrots, even potatoes) all found their way into Grandma's kitchen - via her apron.

While these foods were cooking, that apron could become her "pot lifter" for removing hot kettles and pans from the stove, and as she toiled over the hot stove she mopped the sweat from her face with the tail of her apron.

When meal time came Grandma expertly waved aloft that apron to signal the men working in the field to come for dinner.

As she hovered about the dinner table, passing dishes, she flapped that big apron at the "pesky" flies!

When we grandchildren came to visit, that apron stood ready to dry our childish tears, wipe our noses and to shyly hide behind if we were timid when strangers appeared unexpectedly.

In chilly weather I can see Grandma wrapping that friendly apron around her bare arms, or even throwing it up over her head as she hurried outside on an errand or stood at the open door as guests departed.

Occasionally, when she saw unexpected company coming she hurriedly dusted the chair rings with that ever-ready apron.

Evenings she fed the old hens, throwing out handfulls of shelled corn - from her apron, then she gathered the eggs - also in her apron!

When the day's work was finally done, off came Grandma's "garment of many uses" and she carefully draped it over the canary's cage!

Muriel Razor
Washington County, Kansas

(Editor's Note: Mrs. Razor passed away in January, but had an extensive collection of memories of her childhood days already collected. Permission to use this story was given by her son, Myron Razor.)

## Economy Affected One-Room School

It was 1930 - the year after the crash! Farming communities were struggling with more and harder work to make a living. In their midst the one-room schools were scratching for their very existence. Teachers outnumbered the schools and underbid each other for jobs. Definitely the economy had affected the work and recreation of the one-room school communities. I was fortunate to get a position in a "country" school in this year and I worked hard to keep it.

The young people of the community were starved for evening recreation. For them the school was a place to practice home-talent plays which then brought out the whole community on performance night. The proceeds went to the school.

Since the teacher boarded at a home in the school district, everyone knew where she went, what she did, and whom she dated. But the people of the community also backed the teacher. Their appreciation culminated in the good-time togetherness at the spring picnic on the last day of school.

Verna Gallatin
Marshfield, Wisconsin

# CHAPTER 5: Forces Of Nature

## Natural Enemies

I grew up in the depression years. The drouth and grasshoppers were our biggest enemy on the farm. We tried to raise a garden. The grasshoppers ate that plus destroyed trees, especially fruit trees.

The dust storms were scary. Most of us lived one to three miles from school. We got reports of approaching dust storms like we now receive blizzard and severe storm warnings. One school board member warned us at school and called our parents. My Dad met me a mile from home. Boy was I glad to see him! We barely made it home. It was almost as dark as night. The chickens went to roost.

My folks told me to follow the fence in fog, dust storms, or heavy snow. I had one mile to walk on the road and a mile across the pasture.

I had a ready-made new coat when I was five years old. I did not have another one until I was sixteen years old.

Lois Caldwell
Garnett, Kansas

## The Grasshopper Year

We lived on a farm and raised cattle, grain, hay, chickens and a garden. Crops in general looked promising, just right for a grasshopper invasion. It was 1936 and we were newly married and had hopes of a good year. The medium size brownish hoppers came in droves and cleaned fields quickly with their voracious appetites. I remember a large field of tall corn near roasting-ear stage was devoured to six-inch stalks in less than a week. Men worked long hours to put crops in silos to save all possible. Alfalfa was a favorite crop for them to eat. Summer apples and peaches were eaten from the tree as cleanly as birds could. Harness and pitchforks had to be put inside as sweat attracted their appetites. Holes were eaten in clothing as it hung on the line.

Farmers tried plowing a strip around their fields, did some burning and in a few places put out poison mash. One man herded his flock of six hundred turkeys from farm to farm. The turkeys did a good job on the brownish grasshoppers, that did finally disappear. Some big greenish ones, big as your thumb, then arrived. Their spurs were so big and sharp, they cut the turkey crops, so they didn't make satisfactory turkey feed. Most gardens were eaten up. Fodder and hay crops were scant for livestock. Some sold their cattle for lack of feed.

It was a hard year for farmers, but most survived. Farmers are hopeful souls - next year will be better, so they live in hopes of a better time as they go ahead.

Mary Worley<br>Azalea, Oregon

## Dust Days Humor

Among my more vivid memories is recollection of the Western Kansas dust storms during the winter and spring of 1934/1935. That was during my senior year in high school; as I recall, the entire term was somewhat gritty.

By this time, most of the native buffalo grass had been plowed under, and the plains changed to grain fields. It had been very dry in the fall, and there was very little snow that winter. Whatever crops had grown the previous summer had long since been harvested, and the thin stubble remaining in the fields was not enough to hold the soil in place when the wind blew, which was nearly every day.

It seemed if the wind came from the North one day bringing some Nebraska dust, that it would return from the South the next day loaded with top soil from Oklahoma. Soon the soil was pulverized to a flour-like or powder-like fineness; then a vagrant breeze or a whispering zephyr was enough to shift the dust from one location to another. Thus the topsoil of this part of the Great American Breadbasket spent a lot of time traveling through the air that winter.

The wind-driven, loose, powdery soil penetrated the smallest holes and cracks in buildings and machinery. Some ceilings in houses actually collapsed from the weight of the dust in the attic. The dust drifted like snow, especially around the Russian thistles (tumbleweeds to poets) which were caught in the fences and on the north side of buildings. Many internal combustion engines in cars, trucks and tractors were ruined that winter because so much of the very abrasive dust was sucked into the carburetor air intake and literally ground the bearings and pistons beyond functional tolerance.

When the wind started to build, one could see a wall of dust marching across the plains, getting darker, nearer and larger by the minute.

Perhaps the thing which impressed me the most was the proliferation of tall stories engendered by the caprice of Mother Nature when she released the dust storm condition. Two examples of this gallows humor follow:

Joe: "In the middle of the dust storm yesterday, I had to go outside. On my way to the barn, I saw a gopher digging a hole."

Moe: "What's so odd about that? That's what gophers do."

Joe: "Yeah, but 10 feet in the air?"

"After that dust storm the other day, I found a new hat out in the yard. I picked it up and there was a man under it. I tried to help him out of the hole in the ground, but he said, 'I'm ok, but please just see if you can get my horse to move!'"

There's something positive about a society which can make jokes about a really painful situation such as the dust storms, even as they realize no human agency can do a thing to alleviate the problem.

Rex O. Wonnell
San Jose, California

## Starry Starry Night

The depression and drouth went hand in hand. In fact, the drouth years were a contributing factor to the depression.

During the summer of 1934, with temperatures breaking all heat records, my family carried mattresses outside, and we all slept under the open sky each night for two months. Those mattresses remained out all day, and not one drop of rain or dew brought relief.

Margaret Barkley Johnson
Bloomfield, Iowa

## Fire Frenzy

In the early hours of morning a shout of "FIRE!" split the yet pitch black of pre-dawn. Hustled from the sultry bed of delayed sleep; backs of hands rubbed blurred eyes at the alarm. The relentless heat and drought had kept children and adults from retiring to the scorching beds until cooling midnight came.

While lamps were being lit, this alarming cry continued, coming ever closer to our home. The neighbor shouted, "All hands are needed!" Young ones were to wet burlap sacks in the nearly-dry spring branch nearby and deliver them to adults who were fighting the persistent blaze, which was encroaching upon a blind and deaf couple's two-room log home.

A ten acre field of dried grass, head high to Bud and me, lay in the path of the fire, now contained within the woods pasture of another neighbor. Several homes lay beyond the ten acre field, they would inevitably burn should the fire spread into the field. No rain had fallen for months; day after day the temperature soared.

Pawp (Pop) instructed Bud and me to dress quickly. Never during summer were we allowed to wear shoes, except to church. They were then carried to near the schoolhouse where the Sunday School and church were held.

"Put shoes on, too," Pawp said. "There will be snakes trying to escape to the water. You can wet sacks in the spring branch." This, while hitching his overall galluses and tying his shoes.

Following the coal oil lantern which Pawp carried, we hurriedly crossed the dry grassy field toward the ever-advancing fire line.

Wetting the sacks and carrying them to the firefighters, we spent all the long hours until daylight, when the last of the spotty fires were extinguished by the men of the community. The little log house where the deaf man and his blind wife lived was saved, as were all the other homes beyond the dry grassy field.

Red, smoke-swollen eyes were relieved by the sleep of exhaustion as we spread our pallets under the giant sycamore trees in our yard. Pawp could afford no such luxury. It was haying time at Grandpa's.

> Virginia Snyder
> Bismarck, Missouri

## First Dust Storm

One day my Father was out in the field plowing. In the north we saw something turning black. It was like the whole world was black.

My Mother became frightened as she didn't know why the sky was turning black. I was a little girl. I became afraid and started to cry. My Mother and I wanted my Father.

The wall kept coming closer, rolling big rolls. Just as it was about to hit, we saw my Father just ahead of it. We didn't have a cellar at that time, so we went in the house and shut all the windows. We felt better with Father with us. He was afraid, too, he had never seen anything like this before either.

When it hit, it was black, you could barely see our kerosene

71

lamp burning on the table. Dirt sifted in our home everywhere. We had to cover our mouths with handkerchiefs to keep the dust out of our throats. This one lasted only a few hours if I remember right.

Later we learned this was our first big dust storm on the plains of western Kansas. Our family has been in many more from that first one of the the depression of the 1930s.

Pauline Fecht
Syracuse, Kansas

## Dust Caused Tragedies

People began plowing up most all the sod and making wheat fields. They disced the sod until the clods were all broken and then harrowed it down smooth. Well, the wind didn't stop blowing and we had dust storms. It wasn't unusual.

One nice summer day my husband and two little girls were outside and said there was a storm coming. There was dirt rolling in the air from the north, from the west and the east. He brought the girls to the house and went back and shut the windmill off. It hit and he had to hang onto the fence and follow it to the house because he couldn't see.

We didn't have electricity and I was afraid to light the lamp. It blew for three days. Next morning we went to the barn to milk, we had left the cows in the barn. Three milk cows were dead. They had been choked to death by dust. Almost all the families had dust pneumonia, large amounts of people died with pneumonia.

Still the wind blew all the thirties. But, now people began to plant grass where it should have been this whole time. Now the prairies are getting where they are very pretty.

Fern Jacobs
Rocky Comfort, Missouri

## Insect Invaders

The potato patch was big enough to keep boys busy hoeing,

and fighting potato bugs. An ordinary tin can about a third full of kerosene, and a small stick to knock bugs off into the can by boys took only as long as the boys attended every plant. One could sprinkle the plants with Paris Green, or spray with Arsenate of Lead which has been banned many years.

One other memory of home life on Saturday is when my brother and I helped Dad husk corn in a 20-acre field ravaged by drought, chinch bugs, and grasshoppers. We husked every ear we could find, at the end of the day we only had a half load of undersized ears of corn though we had covered about 16 acres. Dad could have husked a full load in ordinary years in a half day by himself. The chinch bugs came so farmers were told to plow a deep furrow, then drag a pole through it to leave a round smooth bottom onto which they could pour a little stream of creosote to stop the crawling pests. This was called a barrier, and not enough creosote to supply the demand. Dad made the barriers, he got coal tar from the old electric generating plant in Champaign. The chinch bugs became old enough to fly.

Another infestation was grasshoppers. I never realized why they perched upon the handle of a pitchfork beside the barn. They gnawed on the wood just enough to roughen the smooth finish, consequently the handle chafed bare hands.

Emmett Kirby
Champaign, Illinois

# CHAPTER 6: Neighbors And Visitors

## Definition Of A Neighbor

In the depression years everyone was your neighbor. You visited, borrowed, you lended (not money, nobody had any). Whenever anyone was in trouble your neighbor came and helped. You sat up with the sick. You sat up all night with the mourners and the corpse. Nobody was ever alone or in trouble. The neighbors came by foot, by buggy, horseback, and the old tin lizzy to bring food, a handshake, a hug, a shoulder to cry on. Neighbors were neighbors in those days. You did not talk about socializing as they do now. You just came and did what had to be done.

You rubbered on the old party line. Now you might call it snooping. It was not snooping, it was seeing if someone needed help. I was fourteen when my father called the doctor when my older sister was very sick with pneumonia. Within a half an hour our home was filled with neighbors from far and near with food, friendship, concern and any form of help they could give. My dear sister died and they all stayed with us that long night and for days afterwards and how happy we were to have them.

Today I hear people saying "What do I say?" People didn't worry about what to say. They hugged you. They gave you a firm handshake and they just said and did what came naturally. What a comfort they were and how we treasured them!

When my children were small my husband became very ill with pneumonia. I called on the old party line to the nearest hospital and told them I was bringing him in. Chore time came and I had to go home with four toddlers to do the chores. All the way home I worried about how I was going to milk fifteen cows by hand and handle the toddlers. When I drove into the yard, it was full of cars and all the neighboring men were carrying milk pails to the barn. I ran to them sobbing with joy and relief. I cried, "How did you know?" They said, "We rubbered when you called the doctor." God bless them. They did the chores until my husband was able to take over. We tried to pay them and they said, "What are neighbors for?" What a lesson in love and concern and being a neighbor!

Nelle Gilg
Atkinson, Nebraska

## The Watkins Man

We'd see him coming down the road in the late afternoon in his horse-drawn buggy. He planned on having supper and sleeping over at our house. After his horse was fed and sheltered in our barn he and Grandpa would sit on the back porch and sing hymns from the German hymnbook. In the morning after breakfast he'd open the back of the buggy so Mom could select vanilla, pepper, spices, linament enough to last till the next time he came around. Then he'd give us kids a pack of teaberry gum to share, hitch up his horse and be on his way!

Dorothy Bergh
Merrill, Wisconsin

## Riding The Rails

As the months of the Great Depression continued, more and more of the unemployed men of the country began to ride the rails looking for work or simply to keep moving. Lunchtime became a problem for them and that's when our family began sharing sandwiches and coffee with the "railroad bums."

Several times a week during warm weather we would hear a knock on the door with the plea, "Lady, could you spare a little food?" My mother usually said, "All we have is fried egg sandwiches." But that excuse turned no one away, and the transient was soon served an egg sandwich and coffee in his own tin cup, handed out to him.

We began to wonder why we had so many customers. We learned that the riders had a system of marking those houses which were good for a handout. We were one of the marked ones, and though we looked on fenceposts and trees and the sidewalks for some telltale marks, we never found any.

Usually only one or two men came for food, but one summer day we found ourselves with a yardfull of transients. While my mother frantically fried eggs to put on homemade bread, my father was outside holding the floor on the state-of-the-nation. They had to listen. I thought it was a fair trade.

Though most of the men needed a shave or a bath or cleaner clothes, none of them lacked the ability to say, "Thank you."

Dorothy Janke
Russell Springs, Kansas

## Uninvited Visitors

In the depression days my folks often had uninvited company. These "bums" or "hobos" were never turned away. It was a simple matter to share our humble provisions. Mother would fry a couple of eggs, a thick slice of ham, homemade bread and a cup of postum.

On the farm across the road from us a field of cotton was being picked, and was stored in a pile to be removed later. One morning when we had a hungry visitor asking for breakfast, he had cotton in his hair so we knew where he had spent the night.

One morning an elderly couple staggered in for refreshments. Walking was their only means of transportation and they had a long way to go to reach their destination. They were so very tired, dirty and hungry. After a period of refreshment they again trudged on their weary way.

Another elderly man asked to spend the night, but this one didn't seem so "down and out." After bedtime father heard muttering and cursing from the spare bedroom. Father was a religious man so the visitor was reprimanded in the morning. This one had been with us before, but I don't think he came after that.

The visitors weren't always beggars. Sometimes it was peddlers, trying to make an honest living. When these arrived around noon it was taken for granted we would share our meal. They might be selling eyeglasses, chicken and livestock remedies, yard goods, Indian blankets or many other things.

One afternoon our family was enjoying a watermelon break out in our shady yard, and a one-armed man came driving in an open Model T Ford car filled with new brooms to sell. We children were impressed by how he managed to eat watermelon with one hand.

This "entertaining strangers" was taught me from my youth. So after I was married it was still the thing to do, to help the wayfarer on his way.

One Christmas Eve a man asked for a hand-out at our door. The weather was mild and he didn't seem cold, but his thin old raincoat was so very tattered. It being the day before Christmas I was in the mood to make this hand-out extra special, including goodies like candy. Then I thought of his ragged coat. My husband had a wool overcoat that was not new anymore but was still nice. I wondered, should I give him that nice coat? I decided to do so. That night a fierce cold wind blew in. And I was so thankful I had done what I could do to keep him from freezing.

Mrs. Arthur E. Koehn<br>Macon, Mississippi

## The Grass Is Always Greener

One summer morning an aunt was picking with mother and big sis across the road where our place joined a neighbor's. They had on mens' old ragged overalls to protect them from briers, ticks, and chiggers. They were almost startled out of them when the gentle voice of our elderly neighbor spoke, "They are nice, aren't they?" They had decided the berries were better thru the fence and were picking on her land. They were so embarrassed they could hardly answer as they got back to our side. We also gathered and used the wild grapes, hard to pick and sort (I often sorted) but so good combined with apples and made into grape jam for hot biscuits!

Jewell Cooper
Bolivar, Missouri

## Wandering Wood

During the depression winter of 1932 my sister and I lived in a small Nebraska town. Only infrequently could we find employment. We mended, patched and repatched our old clothing, our cupboard was oft-times nearly bare and our house cold for lack of sufficient fuel.

One drab and dreary December evening as we walked homeward from visiting a friend, we spied a large chunk of stove wood laying in a ditch. To whom did it belong, we wondered. It must have fallen unnoticed from a passing truck or wagon. What a fine warm fire it would make! Should we take it or not?

Our Puritan upbringing caused us to hesitate, but briefly. Together we lifted it, carried it home and deposited it on our front porch for the night.

The night was far spent when a slight noise from outside awakened me from sound slumber. I arose and very cautiously peered through the front door curtain.

In the dim half-light of early morning I observed the dark shadowy figure of a man hastily departing from our front yard. In his arms he carried our large chunk of wood.

For several days we pondered the theft of our "prize." Someone other than us needed it, we surmised.

Then one morning we discovered a battered old basket setting on the porch. It contained a generous supply of potatoes, carrots and onions. Attached to the basket was a brief note. It read: "I was passing by and saw the wood. Being out of wood I borrowed it. Am replacing it with these vegetables." There was no signature.

"Well," laughed my sister as we sat down to a noon meal of delicious hot vegetable soup, "cast the wood upon the waters and ere many days it will return to you in the form of carrots, potatoes and onions."

"For which," I added, "we are truly thankful."

Bonnie Holcomb
Urbana, Missouri

## Little Girls' Sacrifice

As a child of the Great Depression, I have many vivid memories. The strongest, perhaps, is seeing two teenage boys, just off a freight train, wolfing down a can of beans and a chunk of bologna on the curb outside the grocery store while I was on my way to school.

I remember the whispered conversations of adults about money - and its lack there of - and how to "make do." That has marked me to this day, I think, for I am thrifty to the point of penny-squeezing, and today's inflation strikes me as both horrible and terrifying.

But for a child, there were happy times, too, sometimes made out of the adults' adversity. I remember considering it a special treat when my father would come home early with his lunch still in its black tin box, and I would help him eat it, myself all unaware that he was home early because the job of day labor on which he had depended had fallen through.

One incident that was both sad and funny concerned my bout with the chicken pox. In those days, the house would be quarantined for a certain period. Since my father wanted to continue working and could not afford to board away from the house, my parents and the doctor did not report my case to the grade school nurse, a real tyrant. (The family of the boy next door did the same when he had whooping cough.)

Inevitably, since there was no word of what really ailed me, rumors began among my friends. I belonged to a group of little girls who called ourselves the "Busy Bees." We met and played and sometimes tried to sew. But the six of us eight-year-olds were very close and my friends began to worry about my continued absence from school.

One Saturday morning a delegation of sad-faced little girls appeared at the door. Considering my infection, my mother could not let them in but talked to them at the door.

They explained that they had heard I had chopped my foot off with an ax! They then presented my mother with a basket of fruit for the invalid. I learned later that it had cost them our entire treasury of thirty-eight cents!

Mother assured them I had not cut off my foot, that I was getting better, that I would be back in school soon, and thanked them profusely for the gift. She knew what a real sacrifice that had been in those penniless days.

Elizabeth Shafer
Colorado Springs, Colorado

## Women Ate Last

Sunday dinners were much like reunions, with all kinds of cousins; first, second, and on down the line. At these big dinners we didn't have paper plates, cups, etc. When dinner was ready all the men ate first, dishes were washed, the children ate, the dishes were washed, then the women ate, washed the dishes and cleaned the kitchen. I often wonder what was left for the women to eat.

Louise Foster
Moberly, Missouri

## "Just Part Of Living"

Another thing more or less connected with food was the constant procession of hoboes that stopped at our house. They got off of the trains when they stopped at the depot, which wasn't far from our house, and then went begging for food. As poor as we were, Dad always gave them something - sometimes just a slice of bread and a glass of milk. If they looked pretty clean, he would invite them in to sit at the dining room table. He would talk to them about where they had been and seemed to enjoy them. I don't remember any of them doing anything wrong or being afraid of them - they were just part of living.

B. Alice Holtsclaw
Hamilton, Illinois

## Fun - Depression Style

Entertainment in the depression era was literary meetings in schoolhouses, and people visiting neighbors and relatives as well as barn dances. The loft floor in the barn would be waxed and the fiddler and caller would get it started. Waltzes, one-steps, two-steps, polkas and schottisches would be performed.

Literaries in the schoolhouse with music - stringed instruments, singing, plays, debates, and readings - were enjoyed.

Neighbors visited a lot and spent enjoyable evenings entertaining themselves with games and conversation.

Agnes Saunders
Wellington, Kansas

## Optimism And Faith

I remember Winfield, Kansas, between 1925 and 1937. The quiet streets tunneled through overhanging elm boughs. Trees and flowers grew in a parkway in the middle of the main street. I remember the parks, shady and green, landscaped with rock gardens and flower beds. Especially I remember Island Park with its moat, bridges, ducks, swans and greedy catfish that churned the water fighting for the crumbs we threw from the footbridge.

Most of all I remember the people, their optimism and faith in the depression. The way they stood together helping each other when the community was battered by dirt storms, grasshoppers,

and devastating floods, one after the other.
Taken with permission from *Travelin' With The Short People*.
> Jeanne Ludlow Murphy,
> Amery, Wisconsin.

## Evening Entertainment

For entertainment Mama had a nice organ and several hymn books. She would play the organ and us girls would gather around and sing. Some Sunday afternoons us three oldest sisters would walk three miles to an elderly neighbor's home and she would play the phonograph for us. It had cylinder records. She had a box full of records and one I still remember was "The Arkansas Traveler."

Our parents had a large Bible and we took turns reading from it almost every evening.

> Mildred Parker
> Alva, Oklahoma

## Next-Door To Bootleggers

Grandma always said that "Hard times make hard people." I believe that is true to a great extent. I think I must have been one of the dumbest brides ever in existence. When I saw our neighbor boy going up the road with a sack on his back many evenings, I wondered. But never once did I think he was "bootlegging." Down the road the other way people moved into a rented place where no one seemed to stay long. I mentioned numerous times as to what a lot of company they had for newcomers, yet I never saw a car there in the daytime. They were from Kentucky and we were amused at some of their customs. But never once did dumb old me ever dream that he made right good liquor! When they moved away I finally learned why the good road into their place, and how they lived so well without working like we did.

In those days there also were chicken thieves. Our brooder house was too close to the road, but it was a seldom used road, and gave the chickens more range. One night I wakened to hear a chicken squawk, and I could see in the moonlight the back end of a car beside the brooder house. I wakened my husband and quicker than I could stop him he was out the door and down the road after that car, yes, in Mother's suit. He was just about a yard from the car when it took off in a spurt of smoke and dust. Boy, was I ever glad to see that car go, and that was one time I was glad he didn't catch the thief.

Flora E. Hay<br>Onaga, Kansas

(Editor's Note: Mrs. Hay wrote this letter to *Capper's* in 1979, but passed away in January of 1993. Permission to use to story was given by Stanley Hay, Onaga, Kansas.)

## Happy Memories

In spite of those hard times of the Depression it seems to me people were much closer in a feeling of community. There was hardly a Sunday that we did not have friends for dinner or a Sunday that we were not invited to friends' homes for dinner. We shared what we had as we shared in experiencing poverty. There are many good memories of those days.

Marvin E. Hanson<br>Boone, Iowa

## Family Reunion

My mother was one of a family of twelve, and the family reunion was always held at our farm home. It was held the second week in August each year. We could see company coming for quite awhile before they arrived. We had over fifty guests at one time. If they were lucky they found a bed to sleep in, if not they slept on the floor. One time my husband, Ed, and I retreated to the bottom of a hay stack, only to have a child make a crash landing, in the middle of his stomach.

Once everyone arrived......chaos! Everyone was either talking, laughing, eating or singing, all at the same time. The children ran in and out of the house, letting a swarm of flies in with each slamming of the screen door. When the flies became so thick we could no longer open our mouths without inhaling one, we would each grab a dishtowel to fan out a swarm of flies, while someione held the doop open for them to go out. It was necessary for us to have the "house fly round up" quite often and we would all join in as we waved the streaming banners of all-white muslin tea towels. I'm sure the flies were laughing as they went out the door, for they knew, with the help of the restless children, that they would soon be back to make a smooth landing on the meringue of a cream pie or for a swim in a pond of gravy.

Marie Rea

Russellville, Missouri

———————■———————

# CHAPTER 7: Making Do

## Recycling the Thirties

No, Virginia, recycling is nothing new under the sun. We just did it so long, we delightedly forgot about it as soon as we could afford to. Now that it is fashionable again, maybe we need a few pointers.

What did we recycle in the Thirties? Everything we couldn't do without. Pans with holes got those wonderful new gadgets called Mendets - rivets with cork and metal washers. If the holes were too large for that, the item became a scoop, an egg basket, or, if large enough, a clothes hamper or a planter, a vegetable bin or a chicken feeder. Only when imagination gave out did you dare throw it away. Then your neighbor would pick it out of the trash and find a use for it.

Old clothes were patched to desperation, then became braided rugs, quilts, dish cloths, mop rags, or patches for something else. Hopeless stockings and socks lost their feet to cushion stuffing, and their legs became rag dolls, double-layered mittens, stocking caps. Aha! You didn't know why they were called that, did you? Shoes took half-soles as long as there remained enough of the uppers to hold them on. After that, they became thongs, hinges for wooden box lids, knee and elbow patches, tobacco pouches. Hand-me-downs were the rule of the day, unpopular though they were. Cut-downs meant shirts, skirts, and jackets for the small fry.

All this is not to mention the popular flour sack, sugar sack, and feed sack. Those items went everywhere in a household. Ripped up, washed, and bleached, they took the place of yard goods for quilt backings, underwear, curtains, dresses, dish towels, shirts, aprons, sheets, pillowcases - you name it and it was made from sacking. They were embroidered, tucked, flounced, ruffled, dyed, stitched, whipped and crocheted around.

A sheet worn in the center was split lengthwise and the outside edges stitched together to form a seam down the middle, then the raw edges hemmed. A sheet too far gone for that treatment, or one subsequently outworn, became bandages, dresser scarves, little folks' underwear, diapers, curtains around recycled orange crates and apple boxes, dust cloths - anything a soft white cloth could be used for.

Sure, tin cans were recycled, too. They made temporary furniture repairs; door stops filled with rocks and covered with scraps of cloth; hassocks when grouped, padded with sock feet or other rags, and bound inside the good part of old overall legs. They made pencil and tool holders, racks for various scatterables, and a wild assortment of toys.

Grease was combined with lye and made into soap. Egg shells, at least in the country, went into chicken feed to extend the oyster shell supply. Table scraps were recycled through hogs, chickens, cats and dogs. Prematurely clabbered milk got cooked into cottage cheese, the whey joining the hog food collection. Stale bread was never thrown out. It made bread pudding, French toast, stuffing, extenders for meats and vegetables, and was often soaked in milk and sweetened for breakfast.

Bent nails were straightened and re-used. Broken harness was used for machine repairs as well as patches for other harness and for door hinges when no others were available. Old tires took on new life as swings, flower beds, "boots" in other worn tires, shoe soles, and door mats. Inner tubes made emergency rubber bands, powered sling shots, patched overshoes, and generally held things together.

Another recyclable was feathers. Never did you pick a

chicken without saving the best feathers for pillows and featherbeds, wash and put them in muslin or sugar sacks, dry them thoroughly, fluff, and you were in business. If the old featherbed had outlived its day, the filling was transferred into pillow ticking or cushions. Good feathers, fluffed and aired, were just never thrown away.

Worn carpets were trimmed, bound, and made into scatter rugs. Woven rag rugs were treated the same way. When a broom had made its peace with the floor, the handle was sawed off and saved for any number of possible uses, including stirring laundry in a boiler, or lard in a butchering kettle, or hanging clothes in a closet. Broken glass was often used to scrape paint.

No, Virginia, recycling is not an invention of the nineties - not by a long shot!

Myrtle Pierson
Monticello, Illinois

## Shoes Were Biggest Problem

I sure can remember the Depression days. My father was a farmer and times were hard. We were a big family of six girls and two boys.

Shoes were the biggest problem. I remember one time Dad went to a shoe sale and came home with about ten pairs of shoes, all different sizes, that he got real cheap. We older girls had to wear high top shoes (old fashion), we really hated to wear them, but it was either that or go barefooted so we wore them. Later when I was in high school, the sole of my shoe wore through, so I cut a piece of heavy cardboard and put it on the inside of the shoe until I could get new ones. (It was hard for my kids to believe this story.)

Emilie Bird
Beatrice, Nebraska

## Fashion Statements

Although it was 62 years ago when I started to high school in the midst of the Great Depression, I can still recall the two dresses I owned. One was blue and orange flowered on a white background. It was ready-made and cost 49¢ at J.C. Penneys. The other was lavender; Mom had made it from a thin material that probably hadn't cost over a quarter. I remember one girl in school who was the envy of her peers. Her father owned a hardware store and had been able to afford the $2.00 dress she wore most of the time. It was beautiful with one part blue with white dots and the other white with blue dots.

During these difficult years a dressmaker friend of mine was kept busy making women's suits out of men's old ones. If she had two pairs of pants to work with, the skirt was no problem, but plump ladies had to forget the whole thing if only one pair was available. This lady was a talented seamstress and the resulting suits a matter of pride to even the most discerning. Her reward for the job? Three dollars and a half.

Marjorie Crouch
Uvalde, Texas

## Soup Kitchens Helped Some

I lived on a small farm in the southern part of Missouri, in the now-famous vicinity of Branson. We worked very hard from early morning until late at night. We had three cows and about 100 chickens, which my mother raised, and sold the eggs and cream to buy the necessary things such as flour, salt, sugar, coffee and lard to supply the ingredients for cooking so we were never hungry.

But in the small towns near us, where the very desperate and hungry were, there was what they called soup kitchens, and they could go there once a day and get something to eat. Mostly big bowls of vegetable soup.

Etta Reiker
Union, Missouri

## Ingenious Parents

In the summer of 1939 my parents went through a brief time

when they were out of cash. When the flour and cornmeal bins became empty they could not be refilled. Imagine trying to feed a family of thirteen without bread. We had cows producing and hens laying, so we had plenty of milk and eggs. There were fresh vegetables in the garden so we were not going to be hungry. But what could we do for bread?

Our ingenious parents were equal to the problem. We would have bread - homemade bread. That was what we usually had. The corn in the field was just past the milk stage - or as we said then - just past the roasting ear stage. Or "roasin ears" to put it in the idiom we used. An older brother was instructed to make a grater from a gallon-size tin can, pounded through with nails, and fastened to a board.

Corn was gathered and shucked. Next the corn was grated into a large pan. It was not an easy job doing so large a quantity by hand. Several of us took turns.

The coarse meal was made into cornbread. Actually it was quite tasty. Some of the kids expressed a dislike for the coarse bread but ate it anyway. We cooked some of the meal for a breakfast cereal. Not the best we ever ate, but filling and nutritious.

Indeed, we were several years ahead of the trends! Our bread was organically grown and unrefined.

Thank God for parents who knew how to cope with difficulties.

Nova Felkins Bailey
Beaverton, Oregon

## Growing Up With *Capper's Weekly*

When I was big enough to remember, we lived in Wyoming out on the prairie. The houses we lived in were frame houses with no insulation. Some houses had nothing on the wall but 2 x 4s. I also wanted to say my Mother papered the lean-to kitchen with *Capper's Weeklys*. Whether they were by subscription or a used one from a neighbor I do not know. We read every word of it - enjoyed the stories and jokes. I remember drying the dishes and reading the *Heart of the Home* letters. I sometimes wonder which shaped the values I have most - *Capper's Weekly* or my mother - probably both.

We made laundry soap out of grease and lye. Mother used an iron kettle over a bonfire. We got our water from a spring near the creek which was about 1/4 mile from the house. So instead of carrying wash water to the house she took the laundry to the spring. Heated the water over a bonfire in the same iron kettle. Washed everything with lye soap a scrub brush on a washboard. When all was done she spread the clothes over bushes to dry in summer. I don't remember how in winter, maybe they froze dry.

Hazel Caruthers
Burlington, Kansas

## Mom's Precious Sacrifice

My clothes were hand-me-downs from my sister or were given to us by someone. I wore long underwear and long stockings for which garters were made out of rings cut from old innertubes.

During those years some people would take shoes that they had outgrown to a room in the basement of the public library uptown. These were given to poor people who couldn't afford to buy new ones – we went there a lot. Usually they found something I could wear, except once.

Surely one of the saddest and yet most precious memories of my whole life concerned my need for a pair of shoes. I can still see my Mom and Dad talking about it - then she slowly removed her wedding ring and placed it in my Dad's hand. He took it to Keokuk, Iowa, to the pawn shop where they gave him five dollars for the ring. He brought home a pair of shoes for me - I can't remember if I ever had a new pair before that time. When I grew up I bought another ring for Mom but I will always remember that she gave up her most precious possession to buy me a pair of shoes. This was our Mom - one of God's finest examples of a Mother.

My dad had a cobbler's last that sat on the floor and he cradled the iron shoe holder between his knees. He resoled our shoes with nails; later bought pairs of rubber soles that he glued on and finally bought soles that had a sticky glue already on them. He also sewed gloves and shoes.

One of my Mom's favorite sayings was, "Dip and deal and save a little for the next meal."

B. Alice Holtsclaw
Hamilton, Illinois

## Early Air-Conditioning

One of my fondest memories of the depression was putting gunny sacks on the windows in the summertime. We would pour water over these. As long as they remained wet, and there was a breeze, we had a coolness to our room. It felt so good on those hot summer days in western Kansas.

If my parents had been the ones to invent the water coolers that we have today; it would have been grand. They had the concept, but didn't keep up with modern technology to invent new products.

My friend tells me her Father used to wrap his feet in rags as he didn't have money to buy himself any socks. My friend was a young bride and her husband wasn't making very much money and they were having a hard time making it. When she saw her father didn't have any socks, this was at Christmas time, she went out and bought him some with what little money she had at the time. From this day on, she always buys men socks for Christmas as she never wants any man to go without socks as her Father did.

Pauline Fecht
Syracuse, Kansas

## Photographic Memories

In the scenes of the Depression Days, like an old photo album, I can see Dad by lamp-light, late at night, sitting on an old stool with the iron shoe-maker's stand between his knees and his lips full of shoe nails; cutting shoe soles from old inner tubes, or sometimes real shoe-sole leather, and nailing them onto our worn-out shoes.

I remember, too, that the next morning, they didn't always fit like they had before. Sometimes we would find tacks sticking our feet. So before we could go to school, Dad had to put the shoe back on the stand and hammer the offending tacks until they were clinched down firmly into the leather.

In the same manner he fixed harness, saddles and bridles, braided cinches and quirts and spliced ropes.

My mother always wore "cover-all" aprons made from flour or salt sacks. She made her under-clothing out of flour sacks, too; as did other ladies in our rural community. (I know that because they exchanged patterns and "how-to" tips.) And all of us girls wore home-made flour-sack bloomers. Colorful printed chicken-feed sacks were a welcome addition, indeed, when they came out.

Virginia Lautenschlager
Hot Springs, South Dakota

## Contentment Found

I was from a very large family and when I was in my teens during the depression days my mother would go to a second-hand store and purchase a bushel basket of clothes for fifty cents. She would then make over and patch things and then hand them down to the next smaller kids as one outgrew things (if they were not worn out).

I never had a store-bought dress until I graduated from eighth grade in a one-room schoolhouse.

We had to go without many things; but we were happy, as contentment is found, not in having everything, but being satisfied with everything we have.

Mrs. James Gray
Rockton, Illinois

## Cedar Chest Produces Dress

As a depression "baby" I have no memories of being hungry or cold as we lived in the country and had a garden, cow for milk, eggs, etc. My memories are of clothes. One always wanted to look as nice as possible.

Mother made many of my clothes from scraps she had or people gave her, also from recycling old clothes. I must have been in the third or fourth grade when we were having a program at school, and Mother decided I needed a "new dress." Money was scarce, so she looked in her cedar chest and came out with a dress of hers, a lovely pink silk. Out of that came a beautiful dress for me, trimmed in blue with little pearl buttons. The only thing new on that dress was the thread it was sewn with. My teacher said, "But Betty, you didn't need a new dress for this." I'm sure I explained how the dress came about. I still remember it fifty years later as one of the prettiest dresses I ever had.

Betty Wortman
Wellsville, Missouri

## Feed Sack Fashions

A new dress was very rare, when we had outgrown the old one. There were no flea markets as most everyone else was in the same struggle.

Print feed sacks were a godsend and we were very thankful for these. Some were very pretty but not colorfast.

We didn't mind if one of our neighbors came to church in the same beautiful print.

I remember the exchange of "How many feed sacks did it take to make that?"

There was also exchanges of feed sacks so as to come up with enough to make a dress of some beautiful print.

Loraine Sands
Lockwood, Missouri

## Curtain Closets

Each summer after I started school when the season was about to begin mother would make me these new cotton dresses and some slips out of flour sacks. Mondays were always wash days, so there was no arguing as to what I was going to wear - only one

93

dress was left in the closet of which the walls were a curtain surrounding the clothes. By spring usually the shoe soles were getting holes in them, but taking them to a shoe repair would be an unnecessary expense so a piece of cardboard was cut and placed inside the shoe and replaced as necessary until a new pair of shoes was a real necessity.

Mabel Nyland
Norton, Kansas

## Make-shift Shower

We built a shower house in the back yard without a roof, using railroad ties for posts and siding from the old house that had been torn down. A curtain stretched across the front, made from discarded drapery. A frame at the top held an old discarded washing machine tub with a shower head attached to the drain hose. A ladder leaned against the side of the building was used to climb on for filling the tub with water a bucket at a time. The water was pumped from a deep well with a hand pump, the tub of water was heated by the sun if it was a clear day, if not, in an iron kettle with a fire built under it.

Marie Rea
Russellville, Missouri

## Scissor Sabotage

My friend told me this story about the depression: she was from a large family. Her mother washed feed sacks, pressed them and cut out and sewed shirts for her boys for school would be starting soon. She cut out underthings for her girls. My friend wanted to have school clothes from the mail order catalog.

One day the sun was starting to set and my friend's mother stopped her treadle sewing machine and said, "There. Soon as I crochet some lace on the bottom they will be ready for you for school, now I must start supper."

My friend wanted mail order clothes so badly. Soon as her mother went to start supper my friend took the scissors laying on

94

the sewing machine and cut holes in the seats of all these pairs.

The mother never said a word, but when school started my friend wore undies made of feed sacks with crocheted lace on the bottom and a patch on the seat of all three pair!

Lucile Hebert
Yucaipa, California

## Preserving Paper

Paper sacks, strings, canning jars and anything else worthwhile was recycled. When I went to college the first time, we were allowed to use both sides of the paper (as I'm doing here). One teacher said if we'd take down his notes, we didn't need to buy a book. I got used ones for about $5.00 a semester, then traded them in to help get the next semester's books.

Agnes Saunders
Wellington, Kansas

## "Making Do With What We Had"

Some men, out of work, wandered the dusty roads laboring for food and shelter for a day, a week, or for however long they were needed. Neighbors traded work, and women assisted each other with gardening, food preservation, making clothing or quilts for the winter.

The work "recycled" was unheard of at this time. We called it "making do with what we had." Women made their own clothing, and that of their family from whatever materials they could afford to buy, or from whatever they had on hand or could trade with some other woman. Many times flour bags were washed and bleached to snowy whiteness to make undergarments. Used clothing was altered or restyled for a "new look," or handed down from one child to the next. Old knitted shawls and sweaters were unraveled and "new" garments fashioned from the used yarn.

The coat I was so proud to wear for two winters was one of my mother's "made over" from my father's army trench coat he wore in 1918. I was the envy of my girl friends at school as I wore this coat with the wide collar which shielded my face from the bitter Kansas wind. The bronze buttons with the eagle imprint, she had polished to a high luster and the wide belt had a shiny metal buckle.

Useable portions of old cotton or chambray garments were saved and cut into strips which were braided together, then stitched to form small rugs. Material from old velvet coats or other wool garments was cut into squares, backed with flannel, and tied with bright cord to make pretty, warm quilts for winter.

Reva M. Smith
Abilene, Kansas

## Dad Worked For What He Received

During the depression one town established garden areas outside of town. A large truck twice a week drove through the neighborhood and men who were not working that day boarded the truck and in the evening returned with a box full of vegetables.

One neighbor of ours with a large family of children spent his time on their front porch with his chair tipped back and his feet on the porch rail reading western novels.

One morning we children watched our dad board the truck and the truck drive on to our neighbor's house. Our neighbor waved the truck on and shouted to our dad, "You are crazy to go work in the hot sun, they will bring you back a box of vegetables!" Sure enough - in the evening the truck stopped and left off a box of vegetables for the neighbors, but my dad said he was glad to work for what he received and could sleep at night with a clear conscience.

Lucile Hebert
Yucaipa, California

## Model T Tantrums

The year was 1928. I was living in northern Missouri when

Mom and Dad packed all of our meager belongings into Dad's Model "T" truck and set out for the land of plenty in central Iowa. Dad had taken a job as a hired hand on a large farm. I was six years old.

It was early spring and although the trip was only one hundred and fifty miles, in my mind it was halfway across country. The roads in those early days were all dirt and in the spring turned to mud.

Dad's overloaded and overworked truck could go no more than twenty-five miles without the radiator heating up. When this happened, the steam came out like Old Faithful and caused the motor to die. Dad knew all of this in advance and carried two, five-gallon cans of water. After the motor cooled down, fresh water was added and then came the swear words as Dad tried to restart the engine.

After all these years I can still hear that truck magnetto making strange buzzing sounds as Dad cranked the engine. The motor would make a few "putt putts" and Dad would run to the steering wheel to advance the spark. After a few unsuccessful tries and some choice language, he told Mom to advance the spark when the motor "putted." Now Mom figured if a little spark advance was good, a lot would be better. This set the stage for the coming attraction.

Dad cranked, the motor "putted," and Mom jammed the spark all the way up. The motor backfired with the sound of an M-80, the crank kicked back, sending Dad sprawling through the mud. The sparks flew, not from the truck, but from Dad.

Mom was trying to keep from laughing. I couldn't suppress my laughter. Dad was mumbling under his breath and wiping mud from his face. Evidently Dad gave up ownership of that truck right on the spot as he called it the son of someone else that I didn't know. Mom never did tell him she advanced the spark all the way up.

Three days later, after umpteen gallons of water, two flat tires, muddy and exhausted, we arrived at our small farmhouse in central Iowa. Dad drove that truck that was the son of somebody else into the farmyard, and as he came to a stop, the radiator started hissing and rumbling and gurgling. All of a sudden there was a terrific explosion and my Dad's pride and joy, his naked woman radiator cap, shot straight into the air. I just know that lady beat John Glenn by forty years as the first person to orbit the earth.

We never did find that radiator cap and once again Dad disowned that truck.

That trip from Missouri to Iowa stands tall in my memory, even after sixty-four years. I gained a very liberal education in English, most of it not in the dictionary, and just think, I hadn't even started school yet. But, that's another story.

Eugene K. Carson<br>Montezuma, Iowa

## "Re-Treading" Tires

Christmas was coming closer each day and father was out of work. He walked to look for work. The tires on the Chevy were worn thin and no money for tires. One day a friend of my father told him he had four used tires in his garage but they were a size larger than what my father's Chevy used. My father did some thinking - the innertubes were good on the Chevy. He accepted the tires his friend offered. He cut the bead off the larger tires and a wheel at a time from the Chevy, used tire irons to put each oversize tire over a worn-out tire. It wasn't an easy job, but when finished they were ready to go.

Lucile Hebert<br>Yucaipa, California

## Twice-Used Twine

Twine or string was a very important commodity in the home. Every little piece was saved, tied tigether and rolled into a ball.

We had no "twistems," no tapes, paper clips, band aids, bobby pins. I don't even remember rubber bands. Twine was used instead. In stores food was purchased wholesale in large quantities, flour came in large wooden barrels (then 100 and 50 lb. sacks) sugar in 100 lb. sacks, as was rice, dry beans, etc.

Crackers and dried fruits came in large wooden boxes. Anything purchased was bought by the pound, put in paper sacks, the tops folded down and twine tied around the package to hold it secure.

What a treat it was to get a small piece of twine to play with! To "whirl the button," or play "One Old Cat!"

A few years later, when some foods were put in cloth sacks, we saved all the twine when we ripped the sack open. There were 1 lb. salt sacks, 10 lb. or 100 lb. sugar sacks, and 50 lb. flour sacks. Later we bought 100 lb. feed sacks. There were plenty of "gunny sacks" for "ripping" when we needed more twine.

Twine was used to hold most anything from sewing strips of rag carpet together to braiding twine into the last few inches of your hair and tying it. This kept the twine from slipping off your braid.

If you stubbed your toe or cut your finger, you wound a strip of white cloth around it and tied it up with a string.

When twine became more plentiful we made baseballs. The twine was covered with denim or soft leather. (The pieces sewed together with more twine of course.) We could play "Andy Over" (over the schoolhouse) for some time, but when the twine sewing wore out, the string inside unraveled and your good times with it were gone forever!

Muriel Razor

Washington County, Kansas

(Editor's Note: Mrs Razor passed away in January, 1993, but had an extensive collection of stories from her life already recorded. Permission to use this story was granted by her son, Myron D. Razor.)

# CHAPTER 8: "These Are A Few Of My Favorite Things"

## "Christmas Comes But Once A Year..."

One Christmas a man from World War I and his family lived close. They had no money for toys, so we hunted around and got some toys. Mom made some clothes and Santa came to their house. An Aunt in Kansas City sent us a 100-pound sack of turnips one year. We peeled and ate them raw. They were delicious. She would send us a box of goodies.

We went to an occasional movie and a circus once or twice. We had a Victrola that we listened to and once in awhile could afford a new record. A popular one was "I Found A Million Dollar Baby In A Ten Cent Store." We went to school functions, band concerts in the park, tent shows, and fishing. My date would come out Sunday afternoons, and we would play dominoes and checkers. We always had a little extra at Christmas. Dad always said, "Christmas comes but once a year, so let's meet it with jolly good cheer."

Cattle were starving by the thousands, so the government bought them. In Gove County, they burned the spines off the cactus so the cattle could eat them and put up green Russian thistles for hay in the winter. We sold our young stock to the government. They slaughtered them and canned them and gave them to the people. For Christmas that year, we made gifts and exchanged them with a neighbor family. I received a box of dominoes made from a cedar post.

> Daisy Massie Scott
> Hugoton, Kansas

## Class Rings For Christmas

Yes, I remember the Depression! My parents had our phone disconnected to save money. I was in high school and that really caused my social life to suffer.

I graduated from high school in 1933. My parents, who farmed, were struggling just to keep up the interest on their farm loan. When our Senior Class began selecting their class rings, my sister and I were told we could not have one - they cost too much. We had to tell our classmates we could not afford rings. There were two boys in our class whose father was a banker. This father undoubtedly knew about the hard times the farmers were enduring. So these boys brought a catalogue to school which featured class rings for $5 a piece. Our classmates agreed on these rings, and my parents said "OK, the rings can be your Christmas presents."

I still have my class ring 60 years later.

> Clarice Morrison
> Coleridge, Nebraska

## Radio From A Bowl

Pictures one sees of Depression Days have usually been gloomy. But they did not appear so to me. I had loving parents and a large group of caring relatives.

There was no radio until I was about eight. Then, family members chipped together and purchased an Atwater Kent with two sets of earphones. My grandmother brought over her large, precious crystal bowl. Into this Pappa put the earphones and carefully placed it in the center of the dining room table. We had all gathered around it as if ready for a feast. Turning on the radio, Pappa began twisting the dials. Suddenly a voice blared out, "WBZ, Boston!" Pappa quickly turned down the volume as lovely music poured forth from the earphones, reflecting clearly from the crystal bowl. We all stared in open-mouthed amazement! What magic!

Jean Carpenter Welborn
Tucson, Arizona

## Gift Memories

One birthday I got a purse with a quarter and pink socks in it. I was very happy. On my very special birthday, my dad baked me a cake, made a freezer of ice cream and three kinds of jello.

A very special Christmas I got a toy bake set wrapped in red tissue paper. I got my hands smacked for shaking the gift before Christmas. Another special Christmas was after World War II had started. I got a dress with a full skirt and a necklace with a small American flag on it. I still have it. Dad had walked to town through deep snow and had carried everything in a gunny sack on his back.

Vera J. Eli
Kansas City, Missouri

## Hunting For Allowance

My father spent most of his short life as a "share-cropper." We only had money in the fall of the year and most of that was owed to some one already, but after crops were harvested he (my father) always seemed to find fill-in work helping to bale hay or feeding out cattle but the money was never enough. None of us boys had an allowance but rabbits were 10¢ apiece and "crows' bills" were 10¢ each so we made our spending money that way. Also, red squirrels were food on the table, but I did not have a rifle.

I found a new .22 bolt action single shot rifle in the local hardware store for $7.95. My father said, "That is a lot of money son and I don't think we can get it."

When it came Christmas morning I did not expect any thing for Christmas. When I woke up and started to take my overalls from the iron bed post, there was the rifle in the pants leg of the overalls. That was the happiest day of my life and I became the best shot in my group and could hit a rabbit in the eye at fifty feet. I'm sure this rifle helped me to become an "expert" in the service with a carbine during World War II. That rifle was in my possession for over sixty years.

Alfred G. Jones
Los Banos, California

## No Lunch For Gifts

I was born in 1921. It seemed all of my early life was in the Depression times. But really people didn't realize it as everyone else was in the same situation.

For special occasions like Christmas I would do without lunch to save the money to buy presents. My brother and his wife and baby lived with us then, and also a single brother. I remember I bought a pair of mittens for my father, a small doll for the baby, and a bandanna handkerchief for each of my brothers. Can't remember what I got my sister-in-law, but it was probably a handkerchief, too.

Della Whitesell
El Dorado Springs, Missouri

## A Family Affair

Looking back on the Depression era, I have many fond memories. Probably the foremost memory is the relationship between us children and our parents, and the warm, loving home they provided.

Families did things together whether it was work or play. They planted the fields, tended them and harvested the crops in the years they were fortunate to have a crop. Families went to ice cream socials and basket dinners at school and after services at the church on Sundays. They went to shivarees, parties at homes and at the school on holiday evenings by lamplight. Families attended brush arbor revivals by the river, Sunday School and church, which were held in the schoolhouse with a visiting preacher each week.

Some of my memories of my family during the Depression era are going to a country school with my three brothers, Mother baking homemade bread, Dad shooting ducks in winter, picking greens (lamb's-quarters) in early spring, making fudge in the iron skillet, having taffy pulls and mother going to club to make quilts.

Glenna Turner
Hardesty, Oklahoma

## Mail Brings $100

Papa and Mamma told us that there just wasn't money for presents for Christmas but we would have apples, oranges, nuts and candy.

My father took two of his half brothers to care for after their mother passed away. They were now grown, one in Washington D.C. with a good job. The other never married and was a wheat farmer in Montana. He would come about every three years to spend the winter with us. We hadn't heard from him in awhile, but three days before Christmas Papa went to the mail box and came in with a letter. He said, "I guess Jim isn't coming, here is a letter from him."

Mother opened the letter and out came a beautiful new one hundred dollar bill, the first one I had ever seen. I got a very much needed warm school coat. I don't remember what the others got but I never had a coat that meant so much to me. It probably didn't cost but six or seven dollars but to me if was fit for a queen.

Viola Wilkinson Bales
Salinas, California

## Whistling While You Worked

No one sings or whistles at work anymore. Always there is a radio or television providing the music that people used to make themselves.

Workers in the fields sang and moved their hoes in rhythm to the song. Mothers sang while they swept the floors or washed dishes. Their music was sometimes off key, but they sang. They sang at bedtime to quiet a tired child.

Men sang or whistled when they walked down the streets. Part of it was for company because houses were far apart. Perhaps some of it was to keep from worrying about the hard times of the depression of the '30s. As a child I thought people were singing because they were happy. Even tho the physical work was hard, people got a satisfaction out of the day's accomplishments and they slept well at night.

Singings were held about once a month in different rural churches, usually on a Sunday afternoon. Anyone could attend and visitors were asked to sing. Sometimes there would be an all day meeting with dinner on the ground.

Gypsy Damaris Boston
Shreveport, Louisiana

## Chocolate-Cookie Christmas

One Christmas I'll never forget was in 1936. I was 8 years old and my brother was eighteen months older. My dad was sick and in the hospital at Norton, Kansas. The doctors thought he had tuberculosis. We had moved to a little house on the edge of Axtell, Kansas, a little town of about 500. The house had no electricity. The City of Axtell had given us a Christmas gift and one evening my mother, brother and I walked uptown to Gaylord's store to get our gifts. One of the items was long underwear. I stood there eyeing the bulk cookie display while Mother visited with the store owner. He saw me looking at the chocolate stick cookies and asked me if I liked them. I said I did - a lot. He filled a sack with cookies for me. This was a real treat because we barely had money enough for food, let alone fancy cookies. Our shopping completed, we walked back to our house. As we stepped on our front porch a lighted Christmas tree suddenly appeared in our living room. Our neighbors across the

105

road, the Alexanders, had talked to Mother and arranged to put up the tree while we were uptown. They strung extension cords across the road to their house so they could light the lights on the tree. There were even presents under the tree. I got the book "Black Beauty." The Alexanders really made a lifetime memory for two little boys. It turned out Dad was only suffering the effects of breathing grain dust at the elevator where he worked, and he was able to come home. I'll never forget our kind neighbors and the chocolate cookies. Once in awhile I buy myself a package of them and I make sure my grandchildren hear this story and get their share.

Gale Polson<br>Marysville, Kansas

## Shoes For Dolly

The teacher in our one-room schoolhouse asked for a volunteer to bring a doll to be baby Jesus in our Christmas play. I quickly volunteered; I was seven or eight years old at the time.

As the day drew near to take the doll to school, I became more and more distressed because my dolly no longer had shoes. Although the doll would be wrapped in a blanket and nobody would see its feet, I wished desperately for the doll to have shoes. After all, I reasoned, the doll was going to be Jesus.

I knew that my mother and father had new Christmas dolls for my sister and me. They were hidden in the icebox on the back porch (my older sister had found the dolls and showed me where they were). I asked my mother to let me borrow the shoes from the doll I was to receive for Christmas for my doll to wear in the play. Then I begged her to let me borrow the shoes. My mother reluctantly agreed with the understanding that, after the play, which was also on the last day of school before the holiday, the shoes would promptly be returned to her.

On the day of the play I was thrilled to have shoes on my doll, all wrapped snug in a blanket representing Jesus in the Christmas nativity.

On Christmas Eve I thought about my doll being baby Jesus

in the school play; then I realized that I had forgotten to bring the doll home from school! In tears I told my mother and father that I had forgotten to bring the doll, with the all-important shoes, home from school.

My parents were upset because they had forgotten about the doll and shoes, too. My father immediately dressed warmly, put the key to the schoolhouse in his pocket and with a lighted lantern left to walk the one-half mile to the schoolhouse on that cold, snowy Christmas Eve.

There was much rejoicing when my father returned to our farm home that night.

Mary Jane Winn Fleming
Gardner, Kansas

## Backyard Birthday

When I was a child, some children in the neighborhood on a Saturday afternoon invited me to a birthday party at their house. I went but did not give a present. There was no money for things other than necessities.

It was early fall and I wondered how they could have a party, they had five children and their gas and lights had been turned off for non-payment, as had ours.

When I arrived in the backyard, near the big walnut tree was a ring of rocks around a small fire and near by a washtub three quarters full of water. The mother gave each of us children a half walnut shell and a small birthday candle. She lit the candle and held our hand and showed us how to tip the candle and drip some wax into the walnut shell and stand the candle in it and float it in the tub of water. Our boats looked pretty sailing on our sea of water in the washtub.

The mother then gave us each a red apple. She peeled our apple carefully, leaving the strip of peel intact. She placed the peel in our cupped hand and had us close our eyes and throw it over our left shoulder. When we opened our eyes we were to identify the shape of the peel on the ground as a letter of the alphabet. That letter was the first letter of our sweetheart's name.

As we ate the apples, the mother made a cup of hot cocoa for each one over the campfire. At that time, if you brought your own container to the local dairy you could have free milk from the processing of cream. If you let it set overnight, cream rose to the top in a small amount. Today it would be called low fat milk. We ate the apple, drank the cocoa, played a game of hide-and-seek and a game of tag. Some happy birthday, and I had a very happy time that is still remembered today.

Lucile Hebert<br>Yucaipa, California

## Cowchips, Not Candy

I was born in 1930 and farmers had very little money then, but my parents always made birthdays and holidays special. My birthday was in January so I was lucky because we would have ice in the stock tank. Dad would chop some ice and put it in a bucket. Mom would make the ice cream custard and put it in a gallon syrup bucket. She would put it in the bucket and we would all take turns turning the syrup around and around. It took a lot of helpers because it made your arms tired. Ever so often we had to open the syrup bucket and scrape the custard off the sides. Then add more ice to the outside bucket and salt. Then turn the bucket some more. It took a long time and the ice cream never got really hard, but when Mom took it out and served it in the long stem sherbert dishes nothing could have tasted better. We always got some small gift. Sometimes a book which was a welcome gift for me because I loved to read. I still have some of my gifts today.

Holidays were special for me, too, but I would bet no one got what we did for Christmas besides our gifts. It all started before I was born. My grandfather had come out from Missouri and brought Christmas candy. My Mother wanted to keep it for Christmas so she hid it in the milkhouse under some gunny sacks next to the potatoes. Somehow my two oldest brothers found where it was and started to take a few pieces each day. My grandpa found out so he put some dried cowchips in a sack and took the candy out. He watched as the boys sneaked into the milkhouse and when they reached in to the sack he was peeking through the door. He said they had a funny look on their faces when they reached in the cow chips. He laughed and laughed till he could hardly breathe. He never let them forget what had happened. So from that joke came the custom of havin' a sack of cow chips to remind us of the times over the year we hadn't been good. No matter how hard I tried to be good the whole year, come Christmas I still got my sack of cow chips. Then we would always laugh over Grandpa's joke.

Marie Holzwarth
Saint Francis, Kansas

## Ethel's Box

As the Christmas season draws near I remember one very special - 1933. It had been a very traumatic year. Not only had it been one of "The Great Depression" but also it had been one of sadness. During the summer my beloved sister, Ethel, had died. She was one of the first diagnosed cases of lymphatic leukemia. Our Mom spent many long hours caring for her, often carrying the very frail little twelve year old girl. Even though I was only six years old I would spend a lot of time rubbing Ethel's legs for the pain that would never go away. After rubbing them I would lift her feet onto small simple wooden box, Ethel's Box.

Christmas Eve of 1933 I out of the clear announced, "I am goin' to hang up my stockin'." A Depression year, no money for essentials let along frivolities as toys or gifts.

Early Christmas morning I ran downstairs, thrust my hand to the bottom of my stocking hanging on the back of a chair behind the old pot-bellied stove. (This was as close to a chimney as I could get.) Racing back up the icy stairs I jumped into bed with my parents to snuggle down and share their warmth.

"What did you find, Annabel?"

"Nuthin'."

I hadn't seen the small doll bed standing in a corner in the semi-darkness. Mom had worked late into the night by the sputtering oil lamp with only the simplest tools, a coping saw, hammer, and her butcher knife to make this Christmas remembrance for her baby girl.

So every Christmas season and other times when I need the assurance of Christmas love I reach out and touch the doll bed - Ethel's Box.

Annabel Walkup
Redding, Iowa

## Graduation Memories

Graduation from high school brings a flood of memories from the depression of 1933. I was the only one of six children to finish the four years. We lived four miles from town, I rode a horse the first year and parked him in the barn north of the school, wore jeans or overalls and took them off in the girls' room as dresses were the usual attire for classes. I walked a lot or caught a ride the rest of the years.

Mother gave me a five dollar bill, which was spent to order a red dress for $2.99 and a jacket for $1.99 thru the catalog. There was no money to get a class ring, Father gave me money to get some pictures made for family. I won a scholarship and used it to go one year to college.

Dorothy Carmann
Riverdale, Nebraska

## Much-Appreciated Gift

I know a Christmas Depression story about a family with three children who bought a section of pasture land and started in the cattle business. The Mother got together a bunch of used coats from relatives and started on a big project to cut patterns and sew coats to warm the three children for going to church and school. It was a struggle using her old sewing machine to sew through heavy seams and really have the garments to look neat for special Christmas gifts for the boy and two girls. Then on Christmas Eve, the husband presented his wife with a brand new sewing machine, (he had sold a couple of cows) and his wife sat down and cried! How she would have really appreciated his gift a few weeks earlier!

Dorothy Carmann
Riverdale, Nebraska

## Remembering Barn Dances

Grandpa and Grandma lived in this two-story small house about a quarter of a mile south of the big white barn where upstairs of the barn the dances were held.

I can remember sitting at Grandpa's feet out on the big rock and cement slab along with some other family members. As the music would begin Grandpa would call my grandmother, who was usually finishing up the daily chores after a busy day.

The sweet music would drift across the orchard and Grandpa would sit tapping his foot, and sometimes would point out the big and little dipper and other star wonders, to my delight.

On occasion we would all attend, but it cost $1 for a couple, dad tells me, and the money wasn't available. I think for a quarter a hamburger could be bought and cold drinks and coffee were a few cents. Sometimes there was homemade pie and cake for just a small charge.

Along one wall at one end there was a couple of old iron beds and small children were placed there as they got sleepy.

No liquor was allowed in the building, but I am sure there were those who went out and returned. Curt (the owner) would ask a person to leave if he felt they were any way out of line.

On some occasions, groups of entertainers from station WIBW in Topeka, Kansas, would be there to sing and play.

There was the outdoor movie where the backs of two buildings and wood and canvas stretched to keep out the freeloaders. When you purchased your ticket you got a numbered ticket and a folding chair. A drawing was held at the end of the serial, movie and preview of the next week's show and groceries would be given to those lucky stub holders.

Also a favorite place when the movie was over you could go

to was Burke's and get a three-dip ice cream cone with a cherry on top for like seven cents.

Wanda I. Smith
Garnett, Kansas

## Homemade Fun

We did have fun and good times during the depression. We usually had relatives nearby and we kids played with their kids. We made homemade ice cream, and got together to eat watermelon we had grown. We exchanged homemade gifts and even had good times working together.

At one time the town drew crowds by having a silent moving picture company come one night a week and showed the movies in an outdoor theater. They were free, and families came and sat in their cars to see them. They were cowboys and black and white. The stores stayed open so they got some business that way. Also contest and entertainments. Our family got the prize of a sack of flour for the biggest family there once. They got us all up on the bandstand. But most of our fun was right there on the farm.

My brothers were clever at making things for fun. They made wooden stilts to "walk tall," and they made pop guns. These were hollow pieces of sticks and then a smaller stick was fitted to be pushed thru the hollow one. They cut bows and arrows out of strong wood. They had "bean shooters" made of a forked stick with strips of inner tubes tied or wired on and a piece of leather to hold the ammunition (usually a small pebble). They made their sleds and they pulled me on one because of my disability as they skated on the pond. They always had inexpensive clamp-on ice skates and marbles and harmonicas. We made some of our balls by unraveling old socks and rolling into string balls. There were cheap rubber balls, too. They made wooden tops by carving them with a notch to wind string at the top.

We had swings hanging from trees, and a cellar door to slide on, a teeter totter was made by nailing a sturdy board on a stump; rather a merry go round.

We could ride hay and grain wagons pulled by the horses. We had picnics in the grove of trees by the pond or down by the branch, and later soon got in the water to celebrate birthdays. We played in the hayloft in the barn, and sometimes took sandwiches up there.

I guess my brothers did not miss having a bike, for few did that we knew anyway. They made a two-wheel cart with a wooden bed to ride in. When taken to the top of the dug cellar, it could take young passengers for a long thrilling ride as the ground sloped clean down to the road.

My brothers made little farms on the ground by fencing off fields and putting board, etc., for buildings. We girls played store by using cracked dishes, empty boxes of household items. The boys also made little tractors and boats by using empty thread spools and rubber bands, with a match to wind up on the end. The boats had a paddle powered by a rubber band and a match wound up.

A lot of fun was just exploring all over the farm, and with cute young animals and poultry we always had, too. We never did get a broken bone, but not because we were not daring. We got plenty of bruises, bee and wasp stings, and sunburns.

Jewell Cooper
Bolivar, Missouri

## Inventive Imaginations

I was raised on a farm in Iowa and was a freshman in high school at the beginning of the great depression. Two brothers and myself were blessed with great "inventive imaginations."

We had no money for movies or other recreation so we devised our own entertainment. We stripped an old unused weatherbeaten buggy down to the running gears only, removed the shaves and installed a long small link chain near each front wheel on the front axle so as to be able to guide it. The "pilot" sat in the middle on the rear axle, holding a chain in each hand and guided it as one would while riding horseback.

We christened it the "Flying Goose" and then proceeded to

113

determine a means of locomotion and came up with gravity as the best means for this overgrown coaster wagon. We pushed it out into a pasture where there was a rather steep long hill and I took the first ride and what a thrill - speeding down this hill, at times having to dodge calves and pigs.

Riding the "Flying Goose" became a popular weekend recreational activity for all the neighbor kids as well as ourselves. Five could ride at one time, one on each side of the pilot, one just ahead of the pilot, and one up front in the middle. What made it so thrilling was there was little, if anything, to hold on to for safety and then of course there were the moving hazards of pigs and calves. Needless to say there were a few accidents, but no serious injuries. What fun we had a little cost.

Francis E. Hager
Phoenix, Arizona

## Circus In The Barn

A fun thing we did was to play in the barn, swinging from the top of the barn on hay ropes and dropping into the hay below. One place we lived we had a barn with doors running through, so we would ride the horses, grab the rail and drop on the next horse. We rode Dad's work horses bareback and this was our circus. (This was only when Mom and Dad went to town!)

Emilie Bird
Beatrice, Nebraska

## Nace's Spring

In spite of what would seem a meager existence to present teenagers, we had a lot of fun. The things I recall best included the summer parties where we played games like "Farmer In The Dell," "Lucy Lost Her Slipper," "The Miller Boy," and "Three Deep." Some were simply running games, but others were much like square dancing without music. Occasionally we had cookies and lemonade if the host family could afford them; otherwise we partied without any refreshments.

The other kind of summer fun centered around a large corner hole in the creek which flowed through our farm. As many as 75 kids have swum or played in it during the day. That we could swim there was a singular blessing we Naces had. The editor of a local paper during these drouth years once wrote, "Fred Nace should get on his knees daily in thanksgiving for the springs on his farm." It was the truth. Not only did he have a fine one in the pasture for the livestock, but he also had the one that more or less kept the water in our swimming hole clean when the water above and below it was green with scum. But oh it was cold! We Naces got somewhat inured to its chilling, but when kids came out from town to swim they'd soon be blue-lipped and shaking.

I'm happy to relate that even grown-ups didn't lose their sense of humor during those terrible days. A favorite pastime was telling about or searching for a giant snake whose trail had been seen in the deep dust in various areas. Opinions ran wild as to its size. I really don't know now if the stories were all "tongue-in-cheek," or if some actually believed such a snake really existed, but the truth finally came out. Some of the men had been dragging a long stacker rope through the dust!

Marjorie Crouch<br>Uvalde, Texas

## Few Gifts For Parents

Entertainment in these depression times was simple, yet afforded fun, laughter, relaxation and good fellowship. Home talent programs, plays, magic shows, and traveling speakers provided opportunities for people to gather and share the news of the day. Usually any gathering such as these was followed with refreshments prepared by the ladies of the area. Occasionally a box supper created a stir among the young eligible bachelors and young women of the community, when girls would prepare a delicious supper, place it in an especially beautiful decorated box, and offer it for an auction, hoping that their "beau" would be the lucky one to get their box. That meant they would share the meal together.

Sunday School parties and neighborhood parties featured sing-spirations in homes or at a church. Winter festivities included sleigh-riding, skating and candy-making parties.

For those who could have two dollars or so for an evening's fun, one could go to a movie for a 50¢ ticket, have a bag of popcorn and have enough left to buy himself, or his girl and himself, a soda, and still have enough gasoline to get to town and home again.

At birthday times, gifts, if there were any, were usually homemade. Dresses, blouses, skirts, and aprons for women and girls, and shirts for the men and boys, and perhaps doll clothes for the little girls in the family. A cake was considered a gift, and homemade ice cream topped the list of birthday treats.

Christmas was a time of joy in our home, even with the poor economy of our country. We always had a Christmas tree cut from the land my father farmed. To our eyes it was always the most beautiful tree in the world, decorated with our paper stars and chains, snowy popcorn strings and ropes of deep red cranberries we'd strung. We did not expect a horde of gifts as children do today, but were delighted when, on Christmas morning, we'd find an apple or an orange and a small toy or candy in the stocking we'd hung the night before. Sometimes there might be a knitted cap or a pair of mittens, or if there was material, a dress for a favorite doll.

Gifts were not always present for the parents at this time. Most parents wanted their children to have a Christmas they'd remember, and to forget for that day, themselves, how difficult things really were, still with a determination to keep Christmas a special time for the family.

Reva M. Smith
Abilene, Kansas

## Catalog Paper Dolls

Christmas time was the usual excitement it brings to children although we were happy doing with much less than involvement of today. Christmas eve was special because as a church group of kids we would bundle up and go caroling. The community was expecting us and would have goodies for us as we were invited in at various places. I recall the year I wanted a manicure set more than anything else for Christmas, but they cost 25¢. I got the set - it was the only gift I received, but I was happy and hadn't expected anything else. Girls I would chum with, and I, had no problem amusing ourselves with whatever we found available to use as a pastime - a favorite was taking the out-of-season catalogs and cutting out paper dolls and then finding the favorite dresses to fit them before the book found its way to the outhouse to do its duty there.

Mabel F. Nyland
Norton, Kansas

## No Generation Gaps

When I was growing up, neighbors got together for dances, both house and barn dances. Young and old went and thoroughly enjoyed each other's company. So different from today when, especially in our small community, cliques are the thing and age groups are distinct. Today the young bunch wouldn't think of dancing with someone not in their age group. Not so when I was young. Young and old danced together and really enjoyed it. I remember so well dancing with my friend's father and even grandfather and having a super time. I think our society is missing a lot by not mingling with age groups other than their own.

Nelle Gaughenbaugh Gilg
Atkinson, Nebraska

## American Ingenuity

Around 1925 or 1926 my father was lucky when he won a console radio in a drawing at Centerville, Iowa, "the only thing he ever drew but his breath," he said. This was the first and only radio in the area, so every evening neighbors came and filled our home, listening to those early radio shows. I still remember many songs popular in that era. My mother complained that our wallpaper had grease spots where young men with their oiled hair leaned back on the wall listening.

I don't believe later generations can grasp what it was like in America during the depression that shaped all our lives for the future. However, there were many happy times and I don't think we knew how poor we were, as we struggled to survive that bleak era. What a wonderful thing the CCC camps were. As well as training young men, they provided a small income to help their families at home. As a result, many projects of this era remained as a monument to American ingenuity.

Margaret Barkley Johnson
Bloomfield, Iowa

## Thanksgiving Tall Tales

One Thanksgiving, all we had for dinner was cornbread and beans. I was too proud to tell the kids at school afterwards, so I told them I had turkey and all the trimmings I could think of. I didn't lie easily and felt like they knew it wasn't the truth. As I think back to those hard times I wonder if some of them weren't doing the same thing.

B. Alice Holtsclaw
Hamilton, Illinois

## Neighborhood Activities

I did many things with the neighbor kids. We played hopscotch, marbles, hide and seek, crack the whip, jump rope, roll the hoop, Andy Over and made hollyhock dolls and bracelets out of white clover blooms. We hung a blanket over the clothesline and put rocks on the corners to make a tent. Nobody had a bicycle but we did rollerskate. We went to the creek under the railroad bridge and fished, swam, caught crawdads and swung on the grapevines, sometimes falling in the water.

B. Alice Holtsclaw
Hamilton, Illinois

## Knives Provide Pastimes

Old men sat on the benches in front of the country store and whittled. Some just whittled on a stick, others made something. It gave them something to do with their hands while they sat and talked. In the hot dry summers of the depression years there was a lot of time when there wasn't work for men to do in rural north Louisiana.

Groceries came in boxes and crates and barrels and cloth sacks. Much of it was shipped on the train. The apple boxes had ends that were perfect for whittling and almost every person had a knife.

Boys might start out with a rusty old cast-off, but as they got older they would find a shiny new knife in the Christmas stocking. A girl might get a tiny knife an inch long with a pearl handle. She was expected to take care of this and use it to sharpen her pencil and keep her fingernails clean.

On a farm a pocketknife was useful. It also provided the pleasant pastime of whittling. Toys and whistles could be made for the children, duck decoys and pencil boxes if you were more talented. The root of the tupelo gum was good for carving.

Someone cut dice out of wood - smooth cubes as large as a woman's thumbnail. A letter was printed on each side of the dice and several sets of dice were made. At Christmastime the letters spelled "St. Nick." At Valentine's Day "Hearts." Young people worked out a system of scoring. As long as you were spelling part of the words you continued to throw the dice. This made a good party game in cold weather. You could set up several card tables. This mixed up the young people and gave everyone a chance to talk to the others.

Gypsy Damaris Boston
Shreveport, Louisiana

## Penny Candy

Saturday was not only a special day because it was a day of escape from school, but it held many other delights.

119

After our weekly bath in the wash tub, we were free to do as we pleased all afternoon. We came for our weekly allowance, "Mama, can we have our penny now?" Even the 5¢ and 10¢ stores are quickly disappearing now. In the days of my childhood, I loved to spend hours looking around our small-town dime store.

Oh, the good things you could buy for a penny! Our noses pressed hard against the glass of the candy counter, we debated whether to buy long suckers, chocolate, butterscotch, round suckers of all colors, or black and red licorice. There were red-hots that would burn your tongue, and bubble gum, and tiny celluloid dolls — before the day of plastic and balloons!

Winnie Krantwashl
Grand Junction, Colorado

## Doll Delight

I have always loved dolls. For Christmas mom made me a rag doll one year. In those days doll heads could be bought for a small price. So Mom got one, made a body and attached it. Made a dress and slip, stockings and a checkered dress out of a flour sack, but the most wonderful of all was a pair of high-topped black shoes with seams so they looked real.

We drew names for Christmas at school. We had no money for that but I'm sure Mom did what she could.

The Christmas Eve program came. The teacher had decorated a tree and to my eyes it was beautiful. Up in that tree was a sweet baby doll about eight inches tall. I just knew whoever had drawn this other girl's name had gotten her that doll. I just knew it was hers, but wished it were mine, and when the name was read it WAS MINE!

Hazel Caruthers
Burlington, Kansas

## Penny Ante

Our neighborhood had a group that got together at the homes

for an evening of "penny ante" during the winter months. Uncle John kept track one winter and he came out ahead eight cents. Lunch was served around 10 o'clock, before all the children got too sleepy. Everyone got a lot of visiting done at those get-togethers.

Dorothy Carmann
Riverdale, Nebraska

## Bucky

Humorous things happened during the Depression. If there hadn't been many of these, life would have been even more difficult.

One episode that the threshing ring in our neighborhood still likes to recall happened this way:

Early in the spring our children raised several "bum" lambs. In spite of parental warnings BUCKY learned to butt - on command! Just clapping hands or slapping one another set him off. While he was tiny it was fun for them but as he grew larger, clapping and slapping were out unless you wanted to get butted down.

On this particular hot August day, the men quit for dinner at noon. The bundle wagons, pitchers in the field, machine men and whoever happened to be at the machine at the time came to clean up for dinner. Toilette facilities consisted of a table, wash pans, soap, kettles of hot water and a towel near the pump in the yard.

The job was a dusty one at best, so as the men entered the yard they attempted to slap some of the dust from their arms and shoulders with their straw hats, before attempting to wash the grime off.

BUCKY heard the slapping sounds and came from the shade of a tree to oblige. Soon the yard was a disaster area, with men tumbling like bowling pins throughout the yard.

The men soon realized what was happening and the humor of the situation, so left the dust on while they waited with straight faces for the latecomers who had scooped grain or had other chores.  They enjoyed a ringside seat for the second performance, which BUCKY was happy to attend, too.  No one was hurt but some dignity was lost by most of the men in the neighborhood.

Ada Hutchens<br>
Harrisonville, Missouri

## The Funny Side

It was in the dark days of the Big Depression and our very first Christmas together.  We had been married less than a year.  I was really depressed.  I wanted so much to give my husband something for Christmas, something that I had bought.  Gifts were cheap but we had absolutely no money.  The few pennies, and I really mean pennies not dollars, that we got for our few eggs and cream had to go for absolute necessities and then often did not quite stretch.  Then to make our holiday season still darker just two weeks before Christmas my husband lost the cherished wristwatch he had received as a graduation gift.

The next time I was in town I stopped in at Mel's second-hand store and there was a wristwatch just like the one my husband had lost.  She wanted two dollars and fifty cents for it. So far as I was concerned she might just as well have asked for a hundred.  I had seventeen cents in my purse.  Then she offered to trade the watch for ten laying hens.  I did not dare.  We had only a few dozen hens and needed them for the eggs, even though eggs were only six cents a dozen.  Then I had an idea.  When I was a child in the lush days of the high world war prices my mother had given both me and a cousin each a lovely bisque doll.  My cousin did not care much for her doll and her early teens gave it to me.  For several years I had really cherished my lovely twins, until my cousin decided she wanted her doll back.  I still had mine but often mentioned how much I regretted losing her twin.  I offered Mel the doll in trade and she agreed.  It hurt to give up the doll, but I had to have that wristwatch and I comforted myself with the realization that the watch would mean a lot more to him than the doll did to me.

Christmas morning came.  I insisted he open his gift first.  He seemed delighted and surprised and yet there seemed to be an odd look on his face as he looked at the watch I slipped on his wrist. My gift was larger, it looked like a large shoe box. I opened it and gasped with surprise. There was my doll.

My husband was beaming and said, "I knew you'd love it. when I saw that doll in at Mel's that looked exactly like your old doll, I couldn't resist it. Get your old doll out of the trunk and let's see if they aren't almost exact twins."

Then we both had to explain. He had never lost his watch but had sold it to Mel for two dollars to buy me a gift and had been carrying those two dollars around for almost two weeks when he saw the doll at Mel's. "It really cost me seven cents," he added. "I had to give Mel a dozen eggs beside the two bucks."

In a sense we had nothing more that Christmas morning, but we both felt a million dollars richer.

Lydia Mayfield<br>Halstead, Kansas

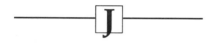

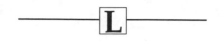

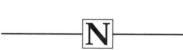

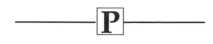

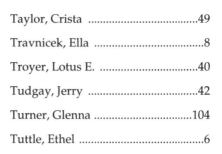